Harry Cole

Policeman's Patch

FONTANA/Collins

First published in Great Britain
in 1982 by Fontana Paperbacks,
8 Grafton Street, London W1X 3LA
Fifth impression January 1990

Printed and bound in Great Britain by
William Collins Sons & Co. Ltd, Glasgow

The views expressed in this book are the author's own
and do not necessarily reflect the official views of
the Metropolitan Police

Policeman's Patch

Harry Cole was born and brought up in Bermondsey, south London. He left school when he was fourteen, during the war, and became a cricket-bat maker, soldier, stonemason and, in 1952, a policeman. For thirty years, until his retirement in 1983, he served at the same police station in London.

He is a qualified FA coach (he has run numerous junior football teams), a referee and a keen cricketer. For many years he had a regular column in the *Warren*, the police magazine. His other books are *Policeman's Progress*, *Policeman's Lot*, *Policeman's Patrol*, *Policeman's Prelude* and *Policeman's Story*, his two-volume autobiography, *Policeman's Gazette* and *The Blue Apprentices*, a novel.

In 1978 Harry Cole was awarded the British Empire Medal for voluntary work. Since leaving the force, in addition to writing he has taken up after-dinner speaking.

To Philip Olds
whose bravery astounds me

Contents

Another Poor Sod You've Killed

Rosie Rafferty would have driven the painter Rubens into ecstasy. She was voluptuous and then some. She must have weighed in around fourteen stone, all of it in perfect proportion. Her cheeks, which were as rosy as her name, set off her flowing hair superbly. She had the small, yet full lips that feature in all of the painter's female subjects. In olden days her torso would have been a figurehead for sturdy men-o'-war. Her proud head, broad shoulders and deep powerful breasts would have provided sanctuary for half a medieval fleet. In short, Rosie was truly magnificent. Unfortunately for me, her thighs, which were easily as awesome as the rest of her, were now resting around my neck, and my back was breaking. Acquiring Rosie's limbs around my shoulders had been no easy feat. In fact, I had been specially trained for it. But at that precise moment I was wishing I had failed the course.

I suppose this is what being a copper is all about. One minute it is a wet November late-turn evening and you are bored to tears. The next you are wondering how you can best explain to your wife how you sustained a high-heeled footprint twelve inches down your back. I was hoping my explanation would prove not only believable but positively praiseworthy. Five minutes before this embrace, I had been driving Mike 3 area car up near the boundary of the Wharf Road manor.

'Just turned half past ten. Isn't it about time we pointed

the car back towards the nick?' hinted Derek Blake, my radio operator.

The area car usually changes over about 10.45 p.m. and we were at the extreme end of our patrol.

'Yes, I'll just drive up to the bingo hall in Foxhill Road. There've been a couple of big winners robbed there recently on their way home.'

The bingo hall was situated in the next street, so all I needed to do was turn left at the 'T' junction immediately ahead. The hall was then a hundred yards down on the left. I slowed at the approach to the junction and finally had to stop as a pink Vauxhall saloon came quickly from my right. I allowed the car to pass and began my left turn. As I raised my vision from the immediate area of the junction, I saw the Vauxhall, about a hundred yards ahead, braking sharply and skidding on the wet surface. The brake lights glared angrily and the car began to slither into the nearside kerb. I could just discern a dark object about eight feet in the air, on the offside of the car. The object then landed in the road, rolled over and over and finally came to a rest on the offside kerbstone. If I had entertained any doubts as to the identity of the object, the screams that could be heard from passers-by soon clarified it.

Rosie Rafferty's bingo evening had gone sadly wrong. Although I had not seen the actual impact, I had observed the speed of the car. Now while it may have been travelling marginally too fast, that did not seem to me in itself the prime cause of the accident. Later, Rosie's first words to me confirmed this very thought.

'I had just left the bingo hall and I was dashing across the road to get a quick Guinness before the pub shut.'

A damning indictment indeed.

As I drove quickly up to the scene of the accident, Derek called urgently over the car radio for an ambulance. Running across the road, we were ourselves almost knocked down by a van approaching from the opposite direction. The sight of a good accident was obviously too much for the van's driver. He drove briskly down the wet street while looking over his left shoulder at the bewildered Mrs Rafferty.

At first glance, which subsequently proved to be correct, Rosie appeared to have sustained few injuries other than a nasty whack to her right leg. She stared down at this damaged limb with a slowly increasing terror. There was no question but that the thigh was badly broken; the whole leg looked like a sleeping python.

'Look at my leg!' she screamed.

It is rare for a policeman to be on scene so quickly at an accident. Usually we are called only second to the ambulance. I tried desperately to remember the treatment for a broken thigh; it did not come very easily.

'We should really try to get those legs together, preferably with some sort of padding in between,' said Derek.

'You're right,' I responded, not really too sure if he was.

Rosie was obviously in tremendous pain. We soon found the only way to bring her some relief was to take the weight off her thigh. We both held the leg firmly in our hands and that seemed to help.

'We'll have to bandage both legs. The first-aid kit is locked in the boot of the car. Can you manage to hold her while I get it?' asked Derek.

'I'll try,' I replied, unconvincingly.

He slowly relinquished his hold but Rosie gave forth another scream as the support for the leg was instantly halved.

'How about if you support her legs across your back?' he suggested.

'How the bloody hell am I going to do that?'

'Well, the kerb's fairly high. If you bend yourself under her legs, you could slowly push yourself up until your

11

back was taking her weight. It'd be worth a try, anyway.'

'Thanks,' I muttered.

I slowly eased my way into the streaming gutter. Between screams, Derek ever-so-slowly placed the two huge thighs across my shoulders.

'That's a lot better, boys,' panted the grateful Rosie.

I soon discovered that what was better for Rosie was infinitely worse for me. My back was killing me. In an effort to avoid placing too much pressure on the injured right leg, I leaned too much the other way. Rosie's left suspender was now scraping my ear.

'I can't very well bind her legs together with your head between her thighs, now can I? You'll have to come out,' ordered Derek irritably.

I wished desperately to say something rude to him but the pain in my back was using up all my energy.

'I'll start on her ankles. Once I've got the first bandage on, you can then slip your head out.'

'We've still got to support her thighs while you bandage them. How are we going to do that?' I grunted.

'You'll have to do that yourself,' he replied as he intently continued to bandage. 'Okay, out you come.'

I slowly inched my way down, until my face was almost touching the wet road. I could hear Rosie becoming more and more agitated. I rolled over, away from the pair of them. Once I was clear, I clambered up into a crouching position. Rosie began to scream again.

'Look, Derek, you hold her thighs, you're stronger than I am. Let me bandage her legs.'

He agreed to this and we slowly changed roles. Although the poor woman was still in great pain, there was obviously some improvement. Her screams had stopped and she nodded and smiled bravely in response to our anxious enquiries as to her welfare.

I had just tied the fourth broad bandage around those

great legs when the ambulance made its welcome appearance. I straightened up with some difficulty and began to explain to the ambulance crew exactly what had happened. Looking down at the patient, I was quite impressed by the results of my first-aid. This was the first (and, I am pleased to say, last) time that I had ever dressed a broken thigh. All in all, I thought I had accomplished a reasonable job. The ambulance driver listened intently at first. He then appeared to stop listening and he crouched down and examined the bandages. He looked up at me.

'Broken thigh, you say?'

'Yes, mate,' I answered confidently enough.

'Well, who the bloody hell done up these dressings?'

Without waiting for an answer, he sliced rapidly through the bandages. He swiftly slipped what appeared to be a large plastic bag on to the injured limb. This he quickly inflated until the leg appeared suspended by air inside the bag. The effect was truly astonishing. Rosie Rafferty sighed and closed her eyes in sheer relief.

'It's magic!' she exclaimed. 'It's absolutely magic!'

Derek began to obtain some particulars of the accident from the still shaking car driver. Meanwhile I accompanied both the crew and stretcher to the ambulance. The stretcher was slid smoothly into the rear of the vehicle and I just stepped in for a last word with Rosie.

'You'll be all right now, Mrs Rafferty. We'll pop round and tell your husband on our way back to the station.'

'He won't be in till the pubs shut,' she said. 'It's not much of a way to spend a thirty-fifth birthday, is it?' she added ruefully.

'Oh, I don't know, luv,' I answered. 'It could have been a lot worse. It might so easily have been your last birthday and that really would have been a high price to pay for a quick Guinness.'

'That's true enough,' she murmured quietly.

13

Suddenly the look on her face changed into quite a mischievous expression. 'Come here a minute, I want to see your nose.'

'Eh? My nose? Whatever for?'

She reached up and touched the tip of it.

'It seems okay,' she smiled. 'After all, there's only you and I know exactly where it's been!'

I waved a fond goodbye to Rosie. I was glad I would not be present when they removed the bag from her leg. I had heard enough cries of pain for one day. I returned to the car where Derek was sitting scribbling away in an accident report book. I knew there was something I had to say very quickly.

'I think I can honestly announce that the minutes I spent between that woman's thighs were among the least erotic of my whole life.'

He looked up from his writing and smiled.

'It's all right, your secret is safe with me. But –' his voice then fell away to a whisper – 'if I was you, I'd wipe my nose before I went home.'

Up to a point that was one of the more successful first-aid ventures of my police career. At least we did not kill the patient and we managed to send her to hospital reasonably intact. For some reason first-aid and I have always been incompatible. Policemen are compelled to sit the exam every few years until the twenty-first year of their service. By that time they are presumed to have reached a stage where they either know it all or are beyond redemption. The relief that I felt when I struggled through that final exam was indescribable.

It has been thirty years since I was at the Metropolitan Police Training School, yet they still refer to my granny knots in awed tones. I never could sort out concussions from compressions. My metatarsus and my auricles became inseparable and as for my ring pads – well, they were a disgrace to the force. My bandages would fall off at the patient's first movement and whatever antidote I prescribed for poisons would always cause the instructor to say cheerily, 'Well, that's another poor sod you've killed.'

The only oasis in this desert of medical gloom was with 'Foreign bodies in the ears'. Now that really is my subject. It would be no idle boast to say that on foreign bodies in the ears I am among the world's leading first-aiders. Although I would modestly consider myself something of a specialist, the reason is unfortunate and one of which I am not proud. Some years ago, on the day prior to one of these infernal examinations, a particularly sneaky individual, who was also being tested, claimed he had seen some of the questions.

'Yours is "foreign bodies in the ear",' he told me confidently.

I had to decide whether to fight him or join him. My abject terror of first-aid convinced me to join him. I spent the entire morning before the exam learning everything about foreign bodies that any first-aider could reasonably be expected to know. Up until that moment, I had known little about the subject. If I had been compelled to guess what it meant, I would probably have plumped for a deceased Ethiopian, up to his patella in someone's earhole. The antidote, I discovered, was to flush it (or him) out with warm olive oil. No self-respecting first-aider would apparently dream of leaving home without such a cure.

On the day of the exam, six of us duly trooped into the examination room. To my horror, the sneak, who was sitting next to me, was asked *my* question! The fact that he also answered it wrong gave me only slight satisfaction. The doctor adjusted his spectacles and looked at the list of names on the clipboard. I waited in trepidation for my question.

'Signs and symptoms of hysteria, please.'

Resisting the answer, 'You've just asked him my bloody question,' it dawned on me that I had just experienced an amazing stroke of luck. I may not have had a dead Ethiopian in my ear, but I was certainly close to hysteria.

'Brought on by mental stress,' I blurted. 'Laughing and crying alternately,' I added, giving another of my own symptoms. 'Clutching at bystanders –' I felt like tearing the throat out of my informant. 'Babbling nonsensical words.'

The doctor looked impressed, as well he might.

'Well, officer, you certainly know your subject, one might almost say well enough to adopt the symptoms. Very good, very good indeed.'

I staggered out of that examination room so confused that I was convinced my police career would only be saved by a hysterical Ethiopian with a lump in his ear.

Later that week, my confidence was dealt its worst-ever blow. I was in Mike 3 returning from Battersea Park where we had been dealing with a huge fight with a motor-cycle gang. One of the participants in the contest was riding his machine just ahead of us. Bootsie Hill, who was then my radio operator, suddenly exclaimed: 'He's losing control of that bike – look!'

The machine had wobbled after hitting a pot-hole and then careered across the road. It mounted the pavement and finally crashed into a wall, throwing the rider into an ominous-looking heap. Bootsie and I rushed to help him. The machine was a write-off and the wall was demolished, yet we could find no obvious injuries to the rider. In spite of this he lay on his back groaning, his right arm fully and rigidly extended. I frankly did not have a clue. Bootsie very shrewdly left me with the patient while he radioed for assistance.

Just then a sweet voice said: 'I'm a nurse, can I help?'

I could have kissed her (in fact I have a recollection that Bootsie did).

'I think he's paralysed,' I whispered.

'Let's have a look at him,' said the Angel of Mercy.

But no matter how we tried, we could not unzip his jacket. However, we did find a very sharp knife in one of his pockets. In a moment of surgical impulse, I cut away his jacket, shirt and vest. Still no sign of any injury. If anything, he became even more rigid. After what seemed like hours the ambulance finally arrived. I hastened to meet it, not wishing the victim to overhear my conversation.

'He's paralysed, I'm afraid,' I murmured to the driver. 'He's totally unable to move.'

Acting on my information, the ambulance crew secured his extended arm with splints and placed him gently in the ambulance. I remember thinking how tragic it was that such a dreadful thing should happen to one so young.

Two hours later, I telephoned the hospital to enquire how he was.

'He's gone home,' said the staff nurse.

'What d'you mean, "gone home"? That's impossible, he was paralysed!'

'There was absolutely nothing wrong with him,' she said emphatically.

'What about his arm, then? That at least must have been broken, he couldn't move it!'

'It was just fright, nothing else. He wasn't even scratched.'

'But I cut all of his clothing away ...'

'Perhaps that's what frightened him. I know it would have terrified me. Actually he wasn't too happy about you, perhaps you should watch out.'

I felt absolutely crushed. They never mentioned anything like this at first-aid classes. The patient was always eternally grateful for having his life saved. It was never suggested that

17

he might leave hospital muttering threats about the idiot who ribboned his clothing.

Guilty though I had long felt about my personal standards of first-aid, it is reassuring to know of the misfortunes of other first-aiders. It is a fact that when a policeman prepares for an exam, a great deal of work is required. This is probably the only period when the average copper gives treatment with any degree of confidence. If, for example, you have just spent three afternoons studying fractures of the tibia and fibula, then it is extremely helpful when the station window cleaner falls from his ladder. Of course, in real life ailments rarely arrive that neatly. It is only on the occasions when you actually *require* a broken leg, that you will receive a strangulated hernia.

Just occasionally, though, some poor soul will be struck by a malady with which you can cope. Oh boy! How good you feel then.

Two of our WPCs, Janet and Bernadette, were on patrol at the junction at Camberwell Green, at the peak of the evening rush-hour. Camberwell Green is a real traffic nightmare. Just one badly parked car can disrupt the flow in all directions for ages. Both girls soon noticed that every vehicle in the vicinity was slowly coming to a halt. The reason lay slap-bang in the centre of the junction. A somewhat scruffy fellow of about thirty years was prostrate and showing no signs of life.

'Sort out the traffic, Bernie. I'll deal with him,' said the eager Janet. The reason for her burst of enthusiasm was because that very morning she had passed her first-aid exam. Her question had in fact been: 'Signs, symptoms and treatment of a coma.' As far as Janet was now concerned, anyone lying still for more than twenty seconds was obviously in a coma. It was purely a question of making the ailment fit the diagnosis. Consultants do it all the time.

Bernie was not overthrilled about her own role in these proceedings. When Camberwell Green really becomes snarled up, the best thing any sensible copper can do is to find a stray dog. Janet was in the middle of the road playing Florence Nightingale and Bernie was expected to divert the traffic around her. The fact that there was absolutely nowhere for these vehicles to go, would be a mere bagatelle for any dedicated first-aider. Janet was determined not to be put off. Gritting her teeth, she managed to turn the patient over on his side, into the prone position. (First rule: 'Prevent the patient from choking.')

She then slipped quickly out of her raincoat and placed the garment over the inert body. (Second rule: 'Keep the patient warm.')

She looked at the pupils of his eyes and, in an effort to find a pulse, held his wrist. She was then suddenly aware of a slight movement from the patient's other hand. It moved very slowly at first. Janet crouched immobile as she watched in total fascination. Was life now flowing back into that languid body? The hand began to reach up in a primeval gesture of gratitude. When the hand had almost reached her chin, it swiftly changed direction – and plunged down the top of her jacket!

At this stage, it may be helpful to state that absolutely everything inside Janet's jacket is real, one-hundred-per-cent Janet. Her eyes and mouth opened wide in total amazement.

'Why, you rotten, randy sod!' she yelled.

Bernadette was engrossed at this precise moment in preventing an articulated lorry from annihilating a mini-van. Her concentration, however, was easily pierced by the words, 'Help, Bernie, he's got my tit!'

With one lightning bound, the 'patient' was up on his feet. He then fled cackling away from the junction, with Janet in determined pursuit. She had dropped a first-class clanger

19

with her diagnosis; she was determined not to drop another and let the bloke escape. After a short sprint, he sank happily to the ground and the fair Janet collared him.

'I love you, missy – and you don't half feel good,' he panted.

The patient was in fact exactly that, a patient. He had walked out of a nearby mental institution and obviously enjoyed his day out. Poor Janet, she was tormented by her colleagues for weeks after: 'Hullo, Janet. What is a hand-up-the-jumper a sign of – a coma or insanity?' Well, all I can say is that if it is a sign of insanity to thrust your hand up Janet's jumper, then half the fellows in the nick would enjoy being crackers!

It would be easy to assume from these pages that the prime function of the Metropolitan Police is to kill all of its first-aid victims. This is of course not so. There are many very dedicated first-aiders in the force. Numerous stations have first-aid teams that compete intently in competitions all over London and the home counties. Scores of people are saved every year by policemen just following a few simple rules. The records of these officers speak for them. The purpose of this chapter is simply to advise anyone not to fall under a bus or have a fit or a baby while I am around.

From my experience, the ability of some officers to deal with potentially serious injuries was best illustrated in a local family feud. New Year's Eve is always a busy night. Casualty departments are as crowded as saloon bars and usually contain as many drunks. Just before midnight the Gregorys and the Wallaces were becoming just a little belligerent. The families had not actually hit it off since Jeannie Gregory, nineteen years of age and a spinster of that parish, had produced twin boys. Jeannie claimed, and it was probably true, that she had no idea who the father was. On the other hand, the twins both sported really large, ugly noses. Now every one of the thirteen Wallaces had really large ugly noses. The local priest, in a vain attempt to pour oil on troubled waters, had suggested a blood test. The only blood test old man Gregory desired was the blood of every Wallace that he could lay his hands on.

Two years had passed since the twins' birth and that Christmas had been surprisingly peaceful. Jeannie Gregory, full, no doubt, of Chirstmas spirit (50 per cent of it vodka), had suggested a New Year truce.

'And why don't we have a New Year's Eve party to celebrate it?' she had naïvely asked.

If the past two years had been like a slowly simmering bomb, then Jeannie had just suggested a pretty good detonator.

I was strolling down the Walworth Road when I heard the call go out via my personal radio to the area car.

'Mike 3 – Mike 3. 92 Eastmacote Street, serious disturbance and assault. Bottles and knives being used. Ambulance called. Message ends, zero, zero, zero, two.'

Zero, zero, zero, two! Absolutely magic! The New Year's Eve truce had lasted exactly two minutes into the first day!

Being little more than five minutes' walk from the address, I quickened my pace. Deep down I was secretly hoping that I would not be first on the scene. I need not have worried; the area car beat me by some seconds. As I turned the corner of Eastmacote Street, I saw the area car screech to a halt from the opposite direction. The two-men-and-one-woman crew leapt out and ran into the open door of number 92. I followed quickly behind.

There was not a chair, cup, curtain, plate or glass left intact in that house. The pools of beer that lay on the floor were diluted with blood. Just above, everyone in the house appeared dazed and bleeding. The only exception to this was an elderly relative of the Wallaces. He sat on an upturned table with a fiddle in his hand.

'What the hell's been going on here?' exclaimed Bootsie Hill, the driver of Mike 3.

'Sure,' said the old fiddler. 'We've had a little bit o' trouble but it's all right now.'

'All right!!' echoed Bootsie. 'It's about as all right as World War Two!'

I gazed around me in grudging admiration. I had never seen anything like it.

'I'll call for a couple of extra ambulances,' said Mary O'Connell, the radio operator, as she ran back to the area car.

'I fink the old lady could do with a bit of assistance,' said a large-nosed, bloodstained youth.

He pointed to a rounded, white-faced woman of about sixty who sat propped against the wall in the corner of the room.

'What's the matter with you, luv?' I asked.

'It's me 'ead. It 'urts,' she said, pointing to the top of her skull.

At first glance I could see no visible sign of injury. She appeared in fact to be the least bloodstained of anyone in the room. The lighting was not too good, however. A single low-watt bulb hung naked from the centre of the ceiling.

I crouched alongside the woman and examined her head. Her hair was easily her most redeeming feature. It was jet black and thick. It was drawn straight back into an elegant bun at the rear of her head. I gently placed my hand on the top of her skull.

'Does that hurt?'

'It's a bit sore.'

I slowly smoothed my hand back across her head towards the bun. I stopped part of the way through this motion when I thought I saw a faint line of blood at the base of her hairline. Yes, there it was! A trickle of blood in a line straight across the top of her forehead. I softly touched the hair at these roots.

'Cor, that *is* bloody sore,' she winced.

It was entitled to be – she had practically been scalped! Before I could move to stop her, she had instinctively run her hand back across her head. The front of her hair simply peeled back.

'Christ, that don't 'arf 'urt now. It's your bloody fault. What've you done, you silly bugger? It was all right till you started soddin' about with it!'

'Problem with the ambulance!' interrupted Mary O'Connell mercifully. 'They are all engaged for the time being. They are sending one just as soon as they can.'

'First-aiders to the fore,' sang out Bootsie. 'We'd better start taking a look at them.'

'If you find one with a foreign body in the ear, he's mine,' I said hopefully.

The three of them spent the next half-hour in that horror house plugging wounds, bandaging lacerations and restricting the flow of blood. I was the general dogsbody, running here and there, rolling up bandages and untinning plasters. Hygiene took a back seat. It was non-existent in that establishment anyway. It was doubtful if there was a germ known to medical science that could thrive either on a Wallace or on a Gregory.

Finally the ambulance arrived. It was not, in fact, the usual London ambulance at all but a St John's ambulance, crewed by a team of three voluntary workers. They all set to work with vigour and soon the whole scene looked like something from a front-line casualty clearing station. The youngest of the St John's ambulance crew was a tiny girl who appeared to be no more than twelve or thirteen years old. She was in fact in her late teens, the little-girl-lost image being fostered purely by her greatcoat. I assume that the St John's clothing store had experienced some difficulty issuing a garment for one so small. They had obviously been able to hack some material from the bottom of the coat but there was little they could do about the top. The collar came up past her ears and linked up with the grey beret that was perched precariously on her head. I could not help thinking that she looked like a tortoise. She scuffled quickly around taking short, sharp little steps. At any moment I half expected to see her turn completely around inside her coat, but, although I watched intently, sadly she never did.

Eventually, all the injured were shuttled to Guy's Hospital, there to join the multitude who were already in the casualty department. I hitched a lift in the area car and we returned to Wharf Road station. True to form, no one at the party had seen anything or wished to press charges against anyone. This time the feud had gone a little too far. The night duty CID then spent the next six hours taking statements from people who had seen nothing and had nothing to say!

On reflection I thought that the crew of Mike 3 had performed really well. In that single disturbance alone, there were at least thirteen stab wounds and seventeen deepish lacerations. No one appeared to have died. However, knowing both the Wallaces and the Gregorys, there could well be three or four of them buried somewhere in the backyard.

My role in the affair seemed to have been one of assistant cook and bottle washer. I had busied myself thoroughly, without ever knowing what the hell I was doing. It was really quite demoralizing. I realized that if my first-aid knowledge had been unable to establish itself at 92 Eastmacote Street, then I was always destined to be a medical duffer.

Because of occasions like that, I reached my twenty-first

year of service with great relief. The thought that I would never have to face another first-aid exam delighted me beyond description. My pleasure, however, was to be short-lived. A few weeks after the exam, my daughter came home excitedly from a Girl Guides' evening.

'Dad, my friend Lyn and I are going to study for our first-aid badges. I told our Guide leader that you are a qualified first-aider and you would coach us at home. Is that okay?'

'No, it's *not* okay!' I snapped. 'You had no right to say that. The first-aid that I deal with is far more advanced than anything you will be expected to know. What will happen is that you will both become terribly confused and fail.'

'Oh, come on now, Dad. A foreign body in the ear is a foreign body in the ear, no matter who is dealing with it!'

How much does she know? I thought. They sounded suspiciously like my wife's words. There had obviously been a family briefing in my absence.

I reluctantly agreed to give professional coaching and soon began to delegate responsibility.

'Right, number one task is for you, Christine. Check and list the contents of our first-aid tin.' (This is an old toffee-tin that lives in a kitchen drawer.)

My daughter returned after something like fifteen seconds with a complete inventory of our family's pharmaceutical treasures.

'Three tins of travel-sick pills and a pair of scissors!'

'Is that it?' I asked in disbelief.

'Ah yes,' interrupted my wife, 'I keep meaning to buy some plasters.'

'Oh, great! What do we do with a cut, then? Bung it full of travel-sick pills and send it on a long journey?'

'Oh you do go on, you know,' she replied. 'Why don't you just set the two girls up with a first-aid situation where they do not need any dressings. Get them to faint or something constructive like that.'

'Okay, Lyn has just fainted and you, Christine, are to give her first-aid. Right, off you go.'

Lyn was immediately seized by Christine and her head brutally rammed down between her knees. After a few moments a horrible gurgling sound arose, followed by the noise of breaking glass.

'Christine! You are not supposed to give sips of cold water while her head is between her knees! You'll bloody drown her!'

I picked up *Girl Guides' Helpful Hints on First Aid*. I read that every good Guide is expected to carry a two-penny piece for a phone call. Once Lyn had ceased coughing, I called both girls to me.

'Why do all good first-aiders carry a two-penny piece?'

Prolonged silence.

'Come now, think about it – surely it is obvious?'

'Is it a tip for the ambulance driver?' said Lyn hopefully.

I looked despairingly at the girl. Suppose you had been hit by a bus. Imagine yourself lying there with eighteen-inch-wide tyre marks on your chest. You look bravely up and see two Girl Guides racing towards you, intent on rendering first-aid. What an incentive to recovery. You really do not have a choice. You get up and run like hell. It could be the greatest recovery since Christ cured the leper.

Perhaps this, then, is what first-aid is all about. It is an incentive to get better quickly. I think of every first-aider that I have ever met, then I wonder just how many of them I would be glad to see if my life-blood was seeping down a drain. Very few. A good gauge of the integrity of a person is the answer to the question: 'Would you buy a second-hand car from this man?'

A similar standard could be set for first-aiders: 'Would

you let him meddle with your metatarsus or tamper with your tendons?'

Only then would we reach a standard where pelvic fractures are treated as smoothly as foreign bodies in the ear.

Suspects on Premises

The heavy spring rain drove into my eyes as I cycled down the Walworth Road. It was 9.40 p.m. on a stormy, dark March evening and the empty pavements only served to emphasize the occasional black umbrella. The lights from the shop windows shimmered in the pavement puddles and amphibious buses swished bow waves over my pedalling limbs. I was about to begin a stint of night duty and I was already wet through.

As I leaned the cycle into a sharp left turn, I heard a very familiar sound from across the road. The burglar alarm at Marks and Spencers was vibrating out its regular nocturnal warning. 'Regular' because each night for over a week the ears of the local residents had been assailed by its incessant ringing. This alarm was in the habit of being triggered off by just about everything except burglars. Rain, hail and winds; cats, moths and mice. If it moved, fluttered, crept, rolled or, sometimes, I swear, just smelt, then off would go the huge bell. Of the hundreds of shops on the Wharf Road manor, the Marks and Spencers of that period was our greatest bane.

There are many shop alarms that I have never heard ring in the thirty years that I have been in the area. Others have become as familiar to me as the bell on my cycle. There was no doubt at all that the whole of the Marks and Spencers alarm system was desperately in need of an overhaul. It was currently top of my nuisance list. We had been assured, in fact, that the overhaul was about to happen. The alarm

28

specialists were due the following week; in the meantime it was 'Bells Across the Meadow' for four hours every night.

The store is so close to Wharf Road police station that it can be seen from our windows. The instant the bell sounds, it is therefore audible to everyone in our building. The thing had begun to ring that night around 9 p.m. and a young PC had nipped smartly across in the rain to carry out a routine check – albeit unenthusiastically.

The manager, who held the keys, was apparently one of the world's greatest socializers. He was never once at home when we telephoned him and was rarely expected back before midnight at the earliest. The one consolation lay in the fact that we were at least dealing with a big store. There could be no doubt, for example, which alarm was actually ringing. This is not always the case with a row of tightly packed shops. Alarms are usually situated high up on the wall between two premises, and often the sound ricochets from surrounding buildings. It is by no means uncommon for a keyholder to be summoned from his bed in the early hours, only to discover that it is his neighbour's alarm that is ringing. It is also a fact that if a person has driven twenty miles into London in adverse weather conditions, often in his pyjamas, he does tend to become somewhat abrasive when he discovers that it is his neighbour's alarm that is cutting through the pre-dawn air.

A few minutes after ten o'clock, the dozen men of the night-duty shift filed out into the Walworth Road. There they separated to the far corners of the manor, shaking hands with padlocks en route. I spent most of the next two hours avoiding the rain. An old copper had told me soon after I joined the force, 'A good copper never gets wet.' I was now not too sure how I fitted that role; after all, I had been soaked to the skin before I had even started.

A little after 12.30 a.m. the rain eased and I relinquished the deep doorway where I had been sheltering. I was due back at the station at 1 a.m. and I was feeling quite hungry. As I turned into Walworth Road, I met my friend Derek, who had been on a distant beat. He was also scheduled for a one o'clock refreshment period and together we headed for the station. Neither of us was too surprised to hear in the distance the still ringing tones of the Marks and Spencers alarm.

'Just listen to that bloody bell,' I said. 'I'm pleased that I don't live anywhere near it, it could send you crackers.'

'It should be okay next week,' he answered, 'they are going to re-wire the whole building. They'll probably have a real break-in then.'

We crossed the road and were just about to enter the station when I thought that I could faintly distinguish a voice between the sound waves of the alarm.

'Can you hear someone calling?' I asked Derek.

He turned, and instantly gasped. 'Look! There's a bloke at that window, on the first floor of Marks and Spencers! He's waving to us!'

'Probably the manager,' I said. 'He'll want us to assist him to search the premises before he re-sets the alarm. D'you know what he looks like?'

'Who?'

'The manager, of course!'

'No, but that bloke doesn't look anything like a manager of Marks and Spencers. He looks more like a refugee from a workhouse.'

We were by this time standing immediately underneath both the window and the bell. The noise was deafening.

Derek cupped his hands. 'Who-er you, mate?'

'Patrick O'Brolly, sur,' came the reply.

'What are you doing up there? You're not the manager, are you?'

'No sur, Oi just came in here for a kip. But der bell is sendin' me mad and oi can't foind me way out, sur!'

30

Derek and I looked at each other unbelievingly.

'How did you get in?' I called.

'Through der door down dere, sur.' He pointed to the extreme end of a line of glass doors that formed the main entrance to the store. At first glance they all appeared closed.

'Well, he couldn't have got in this way,' said Derek. 'They're all clo . . . Oh bloody hell!'

The extreme left door was closed, right enough. It was, in fact, still locked. Where it differed from the other dozen or so doors was in the particular of containing not a square inch of glass! Four hours earlier, someone must have smashed the glass door of the store and then made off. The cursory glance of the young PC had not been detailed enough to reveal the total absence of glass in one of the doors.

Patrick O'Brolly, even in his inebriated state, had been a little more observant. He had found a comfortable, warm, dry, if somewhat noisy haven from the storm. He had climbed the stairs in order to find a quiet place to sleep. Unfortunately for him, he had managed to lock himself in the room just alongside the bell. He had stood the din since the pubs closed two hours earlier but now he had finally cracked. We eventually secured his release and swifted him across the road and into the police station. We satisfied ourselves about his story and he was finally bedded down in the cells for the night.

'Oi just wish it had been Woolworths, sur,' said Patrick before I closed the cell door.

'Why is that, Paddy?' I responded with mild interest.

'Oi moight have found some aspirins, sur.'

Alarms therefore can be excellent as a deterrent (except against the Patrick O'Brollys of this world), but are usually useless for actually catching criminals. But then, I suppose that is not their function. Another drawback to them, besides the cry-wolf aspect, is their ability to lull the property-

31

owner into a false sense of security. The greatest example of this was the Walworth Car Alarm firm which specialize in vehicle security. Unfortunately, they sustained a break-in to their workshop and the suspect made off with £10,000-worth of car alarms. He removed them all from one of their unalarmed vehicles!

No matter how many years a person serves in the force, no matter how experienced he or she may be, the one call that will always cause the adrenalin to flow is 'suspects on premises'! There is something perhaps of the thrill of the chase about it. He is hiding and you are seeking. His instinct is to escape and yours is to capture. There is often an element of danger for both sides. His is the possible curtailment of his liberty, yours is the uncertainty of exactly what it is that you are faced with. I have seen the most cautious of police-men take the most astonishing chances while searching premises for a suspect. I have done so myself. On two separate occasions I have been so intent on the search that I have found myself on a roof with no obvious means of descent. And I'm scared of heights! Both of these ventures resulted in the attendance of the fire brigade to rescue me, much to the delight of my colleagues and the eternal em-barrassment of myself.

Subconsciously, I suppose one is aware of all of the burglaries in which the suspect has got clean away. The sufferings of the victims, the irreparable damage to their property and frequently their minds. To search premises and actually to capture a suspect somehow helps a policeman balance up his mental books. Of course, if it is a house-breaker, then so much the better.

The inconsolable sobbing of the victim comes instantly to mind. Those irreplaceable ear-rings of purely sentimental value; the smashed picture of a dead husband; the excrement on the floor; the urine over the bed; the ripped furnishings; the obscenities carved, or painted, on the living-room walls. The sheer wanton vandalism, demolition and destruction of someone else's private life, often for a few paltry pounds. All of these thoughts will flash through a copper's mind.

The familiar feeling of an anti-climax will, of course, arrive when you discover that the suspect has escaped, or perhaps that he is a Patrick O'Brolly curled up asleep in the back garden. Nevertheless, a policeman needs his 'suspects on premises' shout. It is a fix that will carry him through the next dozen mundane, routine calls.

Because of the uncertainty involved in the searching of premises, no routine can be laid down. Each search is different from the next. Stupid mistakes will be made, inspired guesses will flourish and obvious clues will be missed. On most searches, police arrive separately. They will all tend to look in the same area as each one enters; likewise, they will all probably miss the same area further into the building, assuming that it has already been searched. They will look for a six-feet-tall suspect in cupboards that could not house Kermit the Frog – and just occasionally they will find him there! (The suspect, not Kermit.) They will look in a bedroom for a rapist and not see him. Neither will they see him when he emerges from beneath an eiderdown and calmly leaves via an unguarded window. Two of them will challenge one another in the dark while a third is struggling desperately with an armed suspect on the floor below. They will fall from housetops, window sills and staircases. They will tear their uniforms, graze their elbows and sever their spines. They will tread on newly sewn seed-beds, old fragile roofs and lethal-smelling animal-droppings. They will say, 'I'll never bloody do *that* again!' and they will be the first copper on the scene the very next day.

'Suspects on premises' calls probably excite more nostalgia

among reminiscing coppers than any other single subject except sex.

Not that all of these calls have dramatic overtones; often the reverse. When Derek and I were brand-new recruits, we discovered a side door of a local mission centre that had been left open. It was three o'clock in the morning so we decided to search. The centre was a makeshift collection of old terraced houses, with doors everywhere. Each house had its own exit to the house next door, but always in a different position. There was no communal corridor throughout the dozen or so properties, they were simply linked by a twisting, turning passage. Sometimes this passage led up, sometimes it led down, other times it led nowhere at all. It would lead promisingly through two large rooms, then it would cease at a toilet. Room doors, street doors, cupboard doors were all of the same appearance and design. It was an utter maze.

We spent the next thirty minutes searching the premises and finally discovered a room with a small stage. It was here that the local theatrical group held its rehearsals. We had by this time searched the whole of the mission centre, or so we believed, and we telephoned Wharf Road police station to request their assistance in discovering the key-holder. The telephone was on the lid of a piano which, in turn, was next to a basket of props. While we waited for the station to phone back, we amused ourselves first with the props and then with the piano.

Now while I could never claim to play any musical instrument, I can pick out on the piano a pretty fair introduction to the 'Dark Town Strutters Ball' and 'When You Wash Your Father's Shirt', albeit with one finger. Modest though these accomplishments may be, they are far in advance of Derek's 'The Boers Have Got My Daddy' which sounds like Beethoven's Fifth played with the knuckles. We falteringly played all these renderings while wearing a variety of prop head-dresses. The turban, Viking helmet and Victorian bonnet did little to improve the sound as we reduced each other to giggles. Eventually the phone rang. I picked up the receiver.

'Hullo, Reliance 0081,' I answered, reading the number from the centre of the dial.

'Yes, police at Wharf Road here, guv. It's just to tell you that your premises in Camberwell Road are insecure. We have two officers down there at the moment. Will you please attend and secure the side door?'

The stupidity of the situation suddenly struck me. 'I'm afraid I can't. I'm playing "Dark Town Strutters Ball" in a Viking helmet.'

There was a puzzled silence.

'Is that the keyholder for Cambridge House?'

'No. This is Cambridge House, though.'

'Well, who are you?' said the voice suspiciously.

'Harry Cole. You've rung the keyholder on the number that I gave you to ring me back – you idiot.'

'Well, it's the only number that we've got listed. You'll have to secure the premises yourself, providing you arc satisfied that everything there is okay. Hey! What do you mean – you are wearing a Viking helmet?'

'Well, you see, Derek's wearing a turban and we are giving a concert.'

'Look, get that place locked up and get out of there – and stop acting the fool!'

The click had followed the last word so quickly that it was obvious that old George Rearsdon had slammed down the receiver.

Derek and I restrained our giggles and packed away the props. We were just about to turn off the lights and leave when our attention was drawn to a noise that came from a cupboard in the corner of the room. Our smiles instantly vanished as we moved silently across the room towards the noise. I reached out for the door handle but before I could touch it, it slowly began to turn.

Creaking faintly, it eased open, to reveal the burly figure of a middle-aged man. To our complete astonishment, he was clad in a pair of blue-striped pyjamas, a red dressing-gown and two odd carpet slippers – one blue and the other grey. When the door had first moved, both Derek and I had instinctively reached down to our truncheon pockets. That movement ceased when we saw the newcomer clearly. Burglars, as a general rule, do not attire themselves in such creations.

The man winced at the light and rubbed his eyes with the backs of his hands. 'What the . . .' he began in a very middle-class voice.

The cupboard was now revealed to be a rather compact bedroom. The shaft of yellow light that cut into the darkened room behind him fell upon a sleeping figure in a bed. Corsets and passion-killing drawers were thrown carelessly over a bedroom stool.

'Who are you?' exclaimed the three of us simultaneously. Commander Talbot Brindley-Jones, RN (retired) explained that he was staying at the premises for a few days, at the invitation of a friend who was the centre's director.

'Having a few interviews, y'know. Convenient place to stay.'

Once we had established the legality of his presence, we then swung rather clumsily into our apologies. The Commander instantly cut us short.

'Might have been murdered in our beds! Door open, y'say? Grace must have left it open after she paid the taxi. I'd give you chaps a drink but I don't know where he keeps the stuff.'

'You didn't hear the phone, or the, er, piano?' asked Derek with a casualness that I thought sounded contrived.

'Not a note or a tinkle! Damned fagged out, the pair of us. I only woke up to go to the lavatory.' He turned and looked back into the room. 'Grace is still asleep.'

We finally bade the Commander good night and eventually found the door by which we had entered, emerging once again into the street. The instant the door slammed behind us, I turned to Derek.

'How could he have failed to hear either of us, the piano, or the phone? He couldn't have been more than three yards away from us!'

'Well, there's no doubt he did,' replied Derek. 'He'd obviously just woken up when he came out of that door. Incidentally, I thought you said it was a cupboard! And what about her! She was still asleep all the time that he stood there bellowing. I bet he couldn't find any booze because they finished it all last night!'

'Well, if it makes you sleep that soundly, I think I'll try it myself,' I answered. 'I can just imagine him asleep on the bridge of his ship while the whole bloody fleet sinks around him!'

Searching premises seems to go in cycles. A copper can go weeks without a hint of a 'suspect' call, and then he could have six in one night. The single factor common to each of these calls is that of conjecture: just what will be over that wall, in that yard, on that roof? The suspect could well be the least of it. Could it be an oil-stained, bad-tempered, junk-yard dog? Or perhaps even a goose? Policemen have blithely descended into aviaries, menageries and snake-pits. It is truly amazing what is to be found in some backyards.

The constant clanking of chains in the early hours caused a worried call from a resident at the rear of some shops in the Old Kent Road. My friend Danny Cooke and myself were sent to investigate. A cobbled lane led eventually to a high-walled yard with rather solid-looking gates. We could certainly hear the chain rattling, and the clanks sounded far too heavy to be caused by a dog. In addition, there had been no growls or barks to greet our arrival.

I lifted Danny up and he eventually reached the top of the gate and clambered over. I heard him drop to the ground on the other side. Now Danny had very many attributes, possibly the greatest of these being his command of old English oaths. Within four seconds he had gone through his entire repertoire and had landed back alongside me. His eyes were popping, his chest was heaving and his face was ashen.

'Do you know what's over there?' Without waiting for an answer he exclaimed hysterically, 'A fucking great elephant, that's what!'

'What are you talking about? What's an elephant doing in Simpson's yard?'

'It's scaring the fucking life out of me – that's what it's doing!'

'Well, elephants don't hurt you, do they? I always understood that they were vegetarian.'

'Oh yeh? All right, clever dick – you go over there and shoo it out, then!'

'Well, I'll have a look,' I courageously offered, still not really believing there could be such a creature in Simpson's small yard.

Danny lifted me up with, I thought, a rather unhealthy enthusiasm, and I was soon peering from the top of the gate into the darkness. It took me some seconds to adjust to the almost total pitch. Very slowly, a large, rounded shape began to form. A chain clanked dully and a great head at the front of the shape turned slowly to face me. I may be very much a city boy, but I know an elephant when I see one. I slithered quickly down.

'It's a bloody great elephant!' I panted.

Danny raised his eyes. 'I *told* you it was!'

38

'What's it doing in Simpson's yard?'

'P'raps it's got out of somewhere,' he offered.

'Whadda you mean, "got out of somewhere"? How can an elephant get out of somewhere? It's not a bloody canary! In any case, even if it did, it would hardly lock itself up in a builder's yard!'

We re-examined the gates and surrounding wall. There was no doubt that everything seemed secure and intact. The elephant in the yard was obviously supposed to be there – but why?

We made our way back to Wharf Road station and, after much consideration, decided against telephoning the key-holder. After all, how do you drag someone from bed at three in the morning and tell them that they have an elephant in their yard? If they already know, they are not going to thank you for it; and if they don't, they will simply not believe you.

We left a message for someone from the early turn asking them to call around later in the morning and have a dis-creet word with old Simpson. When we reported back for duty the following night, they had in turn left a message for us. Joe Simpson apparently had a brother who was a part-owner in a small travelling circus. This circus was due to play at nearby Blackheath a couple of days later. He had recently acquired the elephant and there seemed little point in transporting the creature up to Norfolk when the circus's London appearance was so imminent. Joe therefore had undergone a crash course in elephant care and the animal had settled in quite amiably in his yard for the weekend. Unfortunately, Joe had omitted to mention this fact to the neighbours near the yard.

Any disaster that occurs during the searching of premises is frequently due purely to the lack of suitable lighting. The responsibility for this must usually rest with the individual officer. Yet no matter how many times he or she is caught out by this lack of illumination, you can be fairly certain that whenever they start their next spell of night duty their torches will be as inefficient as they were on their last. Perhaps it is just human nature, but torches have for long been my Achilles heel and also, I suspect, that of the vast majority of my colleagues.

In my experience, whenever I had a torch that worked 100 per cent correctly, then I shone it on absolutely everything. This in turn soon wore the bloody thing out and within no time at all I was back to square one with a useless torch. The fact is, I suppose, that if you give a copper an efficient torch, he will shine it.

If ever anyone needed a reliable torch, then Vic Smith and John Plate did when they discovered a break-in in the crypt of St George's Church. This church had fallen into disuse over the previous twenty years and had been boarded up for most of that time. The graveyard had become overgrown and grass and dandelions sprouted from cracks in the outside steps. The once beautiful fluted-stone columns that set off the wide entrance were now covered in graffiti, and the gravel path was a sea of moss.

The church had remained fairly undisturbed during all those years and I, for one, could not remember ever being called there in the line of duty. However, about a month earlier some inquisitive youngster had descended the broken steps at the side of the church and found himself in a deep basement area. With a surprising amount of dedication, he had picked away at a small, iron-barred window, eventually making himself a hole large enough to squeeze through. This hole led him to a sealed part of the crypt. Here, a dozen unnamed dusty bodies had lain inert for almost two centuries. That situation soon underwent a little change. Within a few hours these ancient corpses received their call – not from the herald on the Day of Judgement, but from a snotty-nosed youth during the school holidays. Once inside, our lad had broken open the coffins, scattering limbs and skulls all round the churchyard. This adolescent ghoul had then removed a few rings from chalky-boned knuckles and vanished, presumably returning to his laboratory, where no doubt he kept a monster in a carboy of acid.

It was late evening before the witness to the break-in saw fit to notify the police of the incident.

'Fort I'd do it while I wuz on the way to the pub, guv'nor. Sorta kill two birds wiv one stone as yer might say.'

Although the juvenile Frankenstein had long left the scene, traces of his movements were everywhere. Remnants of bodies led Vic and John to the broken bars like pieces of paper in some macabre paperchase.

The street lights gave the pair enough illumination to gain access to the crypt but once inside it was a different matter. Vic's torch threw a beam for all of three feet, beyond which distance it was like the ocean floor. Useless though this torch was, it would still have been better in John's hands than in Vic's. The reason was that John had a far more nervous disposition. Walking around a deserted, body-strewn crypt would have been trying enough for John on a sunny afternoon in July. On a dark evening in December it was practically paralysing. Having negotiated several obstacles, none of which he could identify, John now found himself somewhere in the centre of the room. He was not really sure of the direction by which he had entered. By the same token, how could he depart?

He had seen neither Vic nor his beam for some minutes now. To call out would have betrayed his terror, yet how much longer could he conceal it? Vic was not, in fact, very far away. Although the bodies may have been beneath the church for a great length of time, Vic had just found something much more recent. Standing on blocks in a recess in the crypt was a small organ. It had apparently been placed there just before the building was closed two decades earlier. The walls of this recess prevented John from seeing the faint glow of Vic's torch. Having now reached the end of his tether, John had decided to contact his partner.

'Vic,' he practically whispered.

Recognizing the thinly disguised terror in John's voice, Vic decided to tease him for a while. He made no reply.

'Vic,' repeated John, a little more insistently.

Again silence.

'VIC!!!'

By way of a reply, it had been Vic's intention to thud down on the organ's keys. He hammered down on them just as the vibrations of John's panic-ridden 'VIC' reached their peak. There was one almighty groan from the organ as the base of the instrument totally disintegrated. Twenty-odd years in the damp atmosphere of that place had been altogether too much for those wooden legs to withstand. The whole thing now collapsed into a moaning musical heap. Vic lost first his torch, then his balance. John all but lost his reason. The language that emitted from amidst the ruins of the organ quickly convinced John of the earthliness of the calamity. Whereas his first impulse had been to stand there and scream, his ambition now was a great deal more tangible: kill Vic!

Somehow the pair struggled torchless into the cold December air. They secured the entrance as well as they could and returned to the station.

The story was recounted many times in the canteen during the next few days. Nevertheless, it was some weeks before the two of them were compatible enough to patrol together in a panda car again.

Compatibility between policemen is, of course, extremely important. If two, or sometimes three people are going to spend a month together cooped up in a car, for example, it is essential that they can communicate. Most policemen can recite numerous instances of crews that worked together for weeks, with barely a word spoken between them. Fortunately these instances are rare and, very often, exaggerated. It is a fact of life, however, that some people are never happy unless they are unhappy. Policemen are no exceptions to this rule.

Take, for instance, a colleague of mine, Iain Gordon, and his friend Tiny. Both lads were extremely compatible but on their shift was a rather dour, miserable Scot named Hamish Brown. Now Hamish was the proud owner of an old-fashioned, 'sit-up-and-beg' Raleigh bicycle. Old it may have been but it was also immaculate and Hamish's pride and joy. Hamish had been posted for the whole of that month to communication duty inside the station. This suited him well because he was never fond of the streets and, to be fair, he was also very competent at administrative work.

By two o'clock in the morning on the third night of night duty, both Iain and Tiny had begun to cast envious eyes at Hamish's cycle. It stood unused and unattended in the station yard, seeming almost to mock them each time they set out on foot around their beats. Iain made several rather half-hearted attempts to borrow the thing because, if nothing else, it would relieve the boredom of his pre-dawn shop patrol. Hamish, though, seemed unmovable.

Tiny, however, was much more persistent. In retrospect, the only conclusion that one can reach is that he simply wore Hamish down. A little after 3.30 on the third morning he could be seen cycling out of the station yard, with Hamish's reluctant blessing. The guarantees that Tiny had been compelled to promise were marginally fewer than might have been needed for a week's hire of an intercontinental satellite, but he was nevertheless cheerful as he set out to patrol his beat and search for his friend.

Iain's first inkling of this coup was when his 4 a.m. peace

was shattered by the sound of a cycle-bell. He turned around, not without some alarm, just in time to see Tiny wobbling around the corner.

'Come on, jump on. I'll give you a lift up to your beat,' sang out Tiny.

The back streets appeared totally deserted as Iain perched himself in the saddle and Tiny bobbed up and down on the cycle pedals.

The couple had travelled less than 200 yards when the noise of an approaching engine caused Iain to turn around. To his horror, he saw a large black police car gliding smoothly along, some fifty yards behind.

'Quick – the Duty Officer,' he exclaimed, tapping Tiny on the shoulder. 'Drop me off here!'

Far from daunting Tiny, the situation seemed to inspire him, and he increased speed. Iain was now clinging on for grim death as the bike gathered momentum down the canal-bank slope.

'Stop, you idiot! We'll break our bloody necks!'

Inevitably, the car caught up with the pair. Iain did not dare to look around into the face of the humourless inspector, who also happened to be a strict disciplinarian. A short tinkle on the police bell finally compelled both riders to turn their heads. To their utter relief, they found not the Dickensian Duty Officer but the area car cruising quietly beside them. Their relief would not have been quite so great had they been aware of the intentions of its driver. Further along the road was a great pile of builder's sand. With perfect timing, the car slowly eased the couple into it. Their helmets went flying as they lay in the sand shaking with laughter.

Eventually rising to their feet, they brushed themselves down and retrieved their helmets. Tiny quickly surveyed Hamish's bike and declared it to be in good working order.

'Just as well, or he'd have killed you!' said Iain, rather happy at the thought of such an eventuality.

The car radio crackled suddenly into life, announcing that a suspect had been disturbed in a block of flats three streets away. Fearing an invitation from Tiny to rejoin him on the bike, Iain leapt into the rear seat of the area car. The car roared away to the location, where a middle-aged lady gave the crew a description of a spotty-faced youth who had attempted to climb into her bedroom. The crew plus Iain then separated and began to search nearby gardens.

Meanwhile, Tiny was making only slow progress towards the scene, primarily because of the amount of sand that now adhered to the cycle's chain. Suddenly, a spotty-faced lad bolted out of a nearby alley and raced away past him. Realizing that it was only four o'clock in the morning and there was no one else about, Tiny felt with some justification that he could have stumbled on to the suspect.

Now Tiny was not the greatest policeman in the world, nor was he an athlete. So it was possibly his inherent sense of fair play that caused him to drop the bike and pursue the youth on foot. Having abandoned the bike, he then proceeded, stripper-like, to discard his raincoat, helmet and torch.

This load-shedding at first seemed to pay dividends, because the gap between the two figures narrowed. As Tiny was just about to nab him, the lad put on a final, desperate spurt. It was all too much for Tiny who was still a little fragile from his cycle ride. As the suspect accelerated away, Tiny's final gesture of defeat was to throw his truncheon after the fleeing figure. It struck him only lightly between the shoulder-blades before clattering to the pavement. The blow did not detract at all from the suspect's speed, and within a few more seconds he was around the corner and gone.

At that stage Tiny gave up. He had done his bit and his energy was now spent. He approached the corner gasping for breath and, as he took in his surroundings, realized that he had chased the suspect around a complete circle.

That figure which was now fast disappearing down the road on old Hamish's bike had been unable to believe his good fortune!

It is not simply the police who can suffer embarrassment at 'suspect' shouts. A local lift-engineer had an experience through an alarm that would fetch tears to the eyes of most men.

Our seedy Wharf Road manor sports little in the way of notable public buildings, although there are several such structures close by on neighbouring manors. Having driven a police van to Paddington railway station to collect a prisoner and two detective escorts, I found myself outside one such building while snarled up in the rush-hour traffic. As I sat frustratedly drumming my fingers on the steering wheel, I was aware of a uniformed security guard waving frantically from the nearby entrance hall.

At that precise moment, a 'suspect' call came over the r/t set, addressed to the local area car and giving that very building as a location. Never throughout my whole police service had I found myself so close to a location when a call was transmitted. The call was not ours, but, with a little rearranging of priorities, I was sure we could manage.

We handcuffed our prisoner to the bench-seat in the van and Detective Constable Keith Simon and I ran towards the waiting security guard. The building itself was a huge ministry complex that had its own security staff. Nobody could enter without a suitable pass or special permission. Certain sections of the building were also additionally alarmed. It was in one of these special sections that the silent alarm had been triggered off.

'No one's allowed in that office. No one at all!' said the guard dramatically.

'Where is it?' Keith asked.

46

'Fifth floor. The lift should be okay now; the engineer has just finished working on it.'

Two minutes later, we hurried out of the lift and along the corridor to room 506.

The whole work force had long since left the building and the cleaning staff were now in possession. Room 506 was a small office leading off the main typing pool. The door apparently should have been locked just with the key in place. Owing to the confidential nature of some of the papers kept in the room, only the supervisor was allowed to enter and clean. That task was usually completed after the rest of the cleaning staff had gone home.

Susan Babington was one of these cleaners. She was a slim, attractive woman whose boyish figure belied her fortieth birthday. Susan had a slight problem. Well, in fact, she had two. The first was Ronald Marlar, the twenty-two-year-old lift-engineer – he was obviously totally smitten by her. The second was Ken Babington, her husband, who was by no means smitten by her, but he was insanely jealous lest anyone else should be. That sort of chemistry accounts for about fifty per cent of all the family disputes that a police officer will be called to – and this one was straight out of that mould.

Each evening Ken Babington would drive Susan the short distance from their nearby flat to the ministry. Two and a half hours later, he would return to take her home. This kind of supervision was effective up to a point, but Susan was by nature a flirt. No matter how closely Ken supervised her while she was coming and going, there was little he could do about it while she was actually there.

Young Ronald had been pouring his not inconsiderable charm on the fair Susan for some months. However, despite the occasional touch, glance and fleeting kiss in the lift, the relationship had not really developed much further. Ronald was determined that it should. Susan, flattered by the

47

attention but easily the more practical of the two, did not see how it could.

Susan's cleaning responsibilities were the whole floor of the typing pool. This she shared with Jean, another female cleaner who worked only two hours each evening, therefore leaving Susan alone for the last thirty minutes. 'Alone' was perhaps not quite the correct word, for it was during this period that her relationship with Ronald had blossomed. Ken Babington had erupted in one of his periodic jealous outbursts just as soon as he had returned home from work that afternoon. It had been the final straw for Susan. She decided that if she were to be accused of an indiscretion then she should at least have the pleasure of committing it. She began to give the evening some careful thought.

Young Ronald wondered what had hit him. He sidled up to Susan after the departure of her cleaning companion and slipped his arm lightly around her waist. She wheeled on him and practically devoured his face with a series of belligerent bites and kisses. She pulled him the short distance into the small office, stopping frequently to repeat her display of passion – or temper.

She had thirty minutes before the supervisor appeared and she was determined to enjoy every second. In reality, she had just three minutes before a security guard, a plain-clothes detective and Constable Cole came hurtling through the door looking for a master spy.

On our entry, Ronald was on the floor having his shirt tugged from him. He did not appear too distressed by this assault, nor did he look much like a spy. He looked more like a young man who was just about to experience a most awful anti-climax.

There are times when no matter how confusing the scene in front of you, you know instantly what is taking place. I did not feel we needed any verbal explanations, the faces told it all. The security guard was not to be put off by any such sensitivity, however. He insisted on every detail. I was then impressed by how frank and sincere both parties were.

'What did you do then?' he would demand.

They would tell him.

After each line of explanation, he would frown and repeat: 'I'll have to report this, you know.'

I frankly could not see why. True, it would be an internal departmental matter, but the results for Susan and, doubtless, for Ron, could be quite severe, particularly if the ferocious Ken ever got to hear about it. There was little we could do to placate the guard, so Keith and I diplomatically withdrew from the scene.

We were greeted at the van by the news that our prisoner was 'breaking his neck for a slash', so we roared away through the now thinning traffic. Just as we left the scene, I saw a car parked on the opposite side of the road. A powerful-looking figure sat behind the wheel, his eyes never once leaving the doors of the ministry.

I just hoped Susan could muster up a good story, otherwise it looked like the police would soon be called back.

Well, one thing was sure, it wouldn't be us – it wasn't our manor and our prisoner wanted a slash.

I Must Be a Policeman –
I've Got a Helmet

Just over halfway through my police service I was asked (blackmailed may be a better word) to become a home beat policeman. This sort of community-cop approach was an attempt by the force to redress the balance by putting men back on to the streets. Much criticism had been made of the increased use of police vehicles. 'You are becoming detached from the public,' the critics cried. That particular interpretation neatly avoided consideration of the enormous increase in police commitments that began in the 1960s. This criticism did, however, have an effect and in 1967 the home beat system was introduced to London.

Now Wharf Road is just one and a half miles from Scotland Yard. It is an extremely busy inner-city station and employs around a hundred officers of all ranks. Yet in spite of this, the station has always been a force backwater. This is never more apparent than when a Wharf Road officer telephones another station – Chelsea, say. The conversation will open as follows:

'Hullo, police station Chelsea. Can I help you?'

'Oh hullo, guv, Wharf Road here.'

'Where?'

'Wharf Road!'

At this stage there is always a silence while the recipient of the call places his hand over the telephone and says to a colleague: 'D'yer know a Wharf Road?' Now if the caller had said 'Brixton', 'Hoxton' or 'Isle of Dogs', the Chelsea copper would have been on to it in a flash. But Wharf Road? It is as removed from him as Saigon, and just about as familiar.

The same discrimination applies to equipment. Whenever an innovation has been brought into the force, then Wharf Road is among the last to receive it. A whole year after the rest of London coppers had brand-new radios, we still sported the old ones. The reception on them had deteriorated to the stage where it was slightly inferior to that rendered by two syrup tins and a piece of string. I could send clearer messages on my whistle.

Raincoats, jackets, shirts and ties. We have always looked a force different from everyone else. There have been occasions when I have felt our station is not listed even at Scotland Yard. The home beat system was no exception. It may have been introduced in 1967 but it took another two years to reach Wharf Road. On 9 April 1969 I first walked out on my own square mile of ground. There, with the exception of events such as marches, demonstrations and riots, I have been ever since.

Perhaps one has more time on a home beat than on any other job in the force. After a couple of days dodging bricks and bottles at Notting Hill and Brixton, it always feels restful to walk slowly down the Walworth Road. The cheery 'Mornin's' from the traders, shoppers and window cleaners are therapy indeed.

The main purpose of the home beat scheme can sometimes be its own downfall. Many people, the elderly in particular, will wait for the local copper when the situation merits more immediate action. One elderly gent watched from his window for two hours while two twelve-year-old boys caused £3000-worth of damage to the local tenants' hall.

'But you are on the phone,' I remonstrated. 'Why on earth didn't you call the station?'

'I did!' he protested. 'But they said you were off duty!'

It had simply never occurred to him to mention the fact to anyone else.

In spite of these obvious disadvantages, it is true that one can certainly get to know people much better; but again, this is not always for the best.

Agnes Beales was a sixty-five-year-old widow who lived alone on the second floor of Nathan House. She would be, in my father's jargon, about the size of a fourpenny rabbit: a tiny woman who appeared tinier each time I saw her. Her height may have shrunk but her tongue never did. Aggie would be delighted to give her views on anything and anyone at any time. Her sister-in-law, Bessie, who lived in the next street, always claimed that Aggie's widowed state was due to her tongue.

'Fair nagged my poor brother into an early grave, she did – God rest his soul. She's a downright wicked old cow. Do you know, Mr Cole, that my mother hated her? And my mother was right!'

Never having known the late Henry Beales, I could not dispute that statement. To be fair, though, the pathologist considered the lorry that had knocked Henry down had more than a passing responsibility for his sudden demise.

Perhaps Aggie needed another target once Henry had died, for most of her vitriol now seemed directed against the estate caretakers. These unfortunate men could never be right. She complained daily about the state of the stairs, lack of lighting, garbage around the rubbish chutes, derelict cars and kids – persistently about kids. There always seemed to be a caretaker either going to, or coming from, 6 Nathan House.

I had just passed the block when I recognized her familiar shrill, cutting tones.

'Per-liceman! Per-liceman!'

I turned to see the little figure scuttling along towards me.

'There's someone calling for help, per-liceman.'

'Where?'

'Up there.' She pointed vaguely to the fourteen storeys of Nathan House. There were four flats on each floor, fifty-six flats in all, each containing elderly single people or married couples.

'Well, don't you *know* where? There's a lot of people living up there, you know,' I said, needlessly.

She shook her head. 'I was just having a chat over there, when I heard it. Clear as a bell it was. H-E-L-P, it went. In fact it went three or four times. Cut right through me, it did. It sounded like some poor soul was in terrible trouble.'

I studied the whole of the exterior of the block for a minute or so, but there was nothing to see. Nor was there anything to hear.

'Have you any idea at all who it could be?' I asked.

'Probably poor old George Bailey on the third floor,' she answered. 'He's got it real bad, you know.'

'He's got what real bad?'

She looked quickly around her. 'Cancer,' she whispered.

'You don't have to whisper, it's not contagious,' I snapped.

'I know, love, but you shouldn't talk about it, should you?'

Feeling that any further conversation with this woman would be a sheer waste of time, I said, 'What number does this Mr Bailey live at?'

'Eleven.'

'Right – let's start there, then.'

Giving a last look at the building, we walked quickly into the vandalized entrance of Nathan House. There was only one lift in the block and that was in use by the milkman. As a general rule, the milkman would take his crates to the top of the flats and descend one floor at a time. He would prop open the lift door with a milk crate while making his deliveries. The lift would thus be effectively out of order for some fifteen minutes. I cursed and began to run up the stairs. Whatever else Aggie may have been, she was certainly a sprightly old girl and she lagged barely a flight behind me.

As I climbed the sixth flight, I began to see the third-floor landing unfolding in front of me. It was in surprising contrast to the entrance-hall below. The lino tiles were polished, the windows were unbroken and the walls graffiti-free.

Number 11 stood silent in the south-east corner, together with a frayed doormat, an unrinsed milk bottle and three mortice locks. I did not wait for Aggie but knocked loudly and officiously on the door. Bending down I called through the letter-box.

'Mr Bailey? It's the police. Are you okay?'

There was at first an ominous silence. I repeated the same words.

This time a weak voice answered. 'I'm coming. I'm coming.'

I was now joined by Aggie. 'It'll kill him, you know. The shock'll kill him.'

I ignored her, as the sound of carpet-slippered feet scuffed the floor on the other side of the fortified door. Bolts began to slide, keys began to turn and, finally, a chain rattled. I drummed my fingers impatiently on the door frame while Aggie stared at me and shook her head.

'It'll kill him, you know,' she repeated. 'You should have waited for me. I would have talked with him through the letter-box.'

My personal feelings were that if my own days were numbered and Agnes Beales called through my letter-box, I would turn up the volume on the radio. Still, she could have a point. I watched with some apprehension as the door slowly opened – and stopped after a few inches. A great chain stretched at right angles across the gap. A tired, toothless face peered around the door. It nodded and slowly vanished. The chain rattled and swung down and the door fully opened.

A pathetically thin rake-of-a-man stood before us. He wore a pair of blue-striped pyjamas that were at least four sizes too large. Sagging at the shoulders and waist, they concertina'd over his ankles and obliterated his hands. He took at least three deep breaths and asked faintly, 'Yes?'

'I'm very sorry to trouble you, Mr Bailey, but did you call for help? Mrs Beales thinks perhaps you may have done.'

'Mrs Beales . . .' he panted, and clung on to the framework of the door. He began again and this time appeared to be making a supreme effort. 'Mrs Beales . . . never got anything right . . . Never . . . not in her whole life she didn't . . .' Again a tremendous fight for breath. 'I'm all right . . . I'm going back to bed . . . Thank you all the same . . . 'Bye.'

He slowly closed the door. The keys turned, the bolts slid and the chain rattled.

'Right, then,' I said, turning back to Aggie. 'Where now?'

'Could be him up on the twelfth floor. I don't know his name but he lives in the corner and has fits.'

The lift was now mercifully free, so we were soon on the twelfth floor. This time, although I again knocked, I left it to Aggie to call through the letter-box.

'Yooou – oou,' she sang. 'Mister, er, Mister Wassa-name. Yooou – oou!'

Mister 'Wassa-name' in fact came very quickly to the door. No, it wasn't he who had cried for help. Yes, he had heard the cry himself. He had in fact heard it three times. Although the voice had been most certainly a man's Mister Wassa-name did not recognize it. Nor could he place the direction from which the voice had originated.

Well, this was at least something. There certainly now appeared to have been a definite cry for help.

'Any idea who it could be?' I asked.

'Probably Bernie Spriggs on the ninth floor. His health isn't good and he is always falling about.'

The three of us then piled into the still vacant lift and descended to the ninth. Bernie Spriggs was fixing a new door-bell when the lift opened and our trio stepped out.

'Hullo!' greeted Bernie cheerfully. 'What's going on, then?'

'Are you all right, Mr Spriggs?' I asked.

'Fine. Why, shouldn't I be?'

Mister Wassa-name explained our presence. Bernie then looked thoughtful and said that he thought we would be usefully employed by checking with Mr Devonshire on the third floor.

Then I decided that the whole thing had now gone far enough. At this rate, if I took any notice of Aggie and her associates, we would spend the day running about all over the block, trying to trace a person who I was not even sure existed.

'Right, we'll start at the top and work our way down. We'll knock on every door and keep a list of those from whom we receive no answer. We'll be here for the rest of the week otherwise.'

Together with Aggie, Bernie and Mister Wassa-name I took the lift to the top floor. While I pounded on the door of number 56, my fellow-travellers hit 55, 54 and 53. The majority of tenants were not at home but those who were, joined us. Not only did they join us but they all were convinced that they knew the person in need of help. As we slowly descended the block, so we gathered people. I felt like the Pied Piper. By the time we reached the sixth floor, we had amassed a group of people stretching away from each landing and halfway up the staircase. Occasionally we would meet someone who had actually heard the call. Mostly though, they simply knew someone who might have called.

'No, it wasn't me. It'll probably be Fred Goodbody on the ninth floor.'

'No, it's not! I'm here!' Fred would respond from the staircase.

'Well, have you tried Mary Hackett on the eleventh?'

So it went on, floor after floor, until we reached the third. The supporters behind us had now grown to almost a score. Suddenly, panting up the staircase came a uniformed caretaker. He ran straight to me and gasped, 'There's someone calling for help!'

'Amazing!' I answered, with about as much sarcasm as I could muster. 'And of course you never noticed where he was?'

'Yes, I did!' he exclaimed indignantly. 'He was on the second floor.'

'The second floor? That's impossible!' retorted Aggie. 'There's nobody in on the second floor, I live there myself. Everyone is out except me.'

'I tell you I saw him! He had overalls on and curly hair.'

For the first time doubt showed on Aggie's face.

'W-e-l-l,' she faltered. 'There should be a plumber in my kitchen. I wonder if perhaps . . . ?'

Waiting no longer, I ran down the two flights of stairs to the floor below. Three of the flats' doors were closed but the remaining one, number 6, was slightly ajar.

'H-E-L-P,' came the muffled cry.

I pushed open the door and sprinted along the passage.

Again a muffled 'H-E-L-P'.

I charged into the living-room, colliding with a couple of chairs en route, but I could neither see nor hear anything unusual. I stood silent for a moment.

'Where are you?' I called.

'Kitchen!' came the curt reply.

Rushing into the kitchen, my first impression was one of an empty room. On closer inspection, however, I saw a fair-haired young man in blue overalls curled up under the sink unit. He looked extremely uncomfortable and sweat poured from his brow.

'Fank Gawd someone's turned up!' he panted. 'Can you hold this for a minute?'

Both his hands were clutched tightly around a hot-water pipe. The pipe appeared to be broken at a point near the wall. I gradually took over from him and for the first time noticed the large pool of water on the floor. The plumber momentarily disappeared into a large immersion cupboard, as the first of my entourage appeared at the door. The second was Agnes herself.

'What on earth are you doing, per-liceman?'

'To the best of my knowledge, I'm holding your bloody hot-water pipe in place. I know it's your *hot*-water pipe because my skin is burning.'

'*Your* skin is burning? How d'yer fink I feel?' said the emerging plumber. 'And where the bloody 'ell 'ave you been?'

The last remark was addressed to Agnes almost as a threat.

'Er – well, I – er, just slipped out,' she wavered. 'I thought you were managing all right and I just popped out for a chat.'

'But you told me you were goin' to stay in! I fort you were in the other room and I spent ten minutes calling out to you before I realized that you'd gorn!'

'Look!' I interrupted. 'Do you mind if I let this pipe go? It's bloody hot!'

'Oh yes, mate, sorry. I forgot about you. I've turned the 'ot water off at the immersion. It'll be okay now.'

Just then the estate caretaker decided it was time he made his presence felt.

'Are you telling us that this cry for help that we've all

been rushing about all over the sodding place for was from your own flat?'

'Well, yes, but I wasn't to know, was I?' pleaded Aggie. 'I mean, after all, it could have come from anywhere in the block, couldn't it?'

'No, it couldn't! It had to come from here,' he persisted. 'You've had the plumbers here so often that it's like a School of Building!'

'That's right!' joined in the plumber. 'I fort you were 'ere. When I realized you wasn't, I ran across to the window and called for 'elp. I couldn't stay there long otherwise all the flats in the floor below would have been flooded out!'

'Wait a minute,' I said. 'Let me get this straight. Are you saying that you let go of the pipe and then ran to the window and called for help?'

'Yeh.'

'You then ran back into the kitchen to hold the pipe?'

'Yeh.'

'So every time anyone looked up to see where the call came from, you'd be on your way back under the sink?'

'Well, yeh.'

I turned to Aggie. 'And you heard a yell for help coming from your own flat and didn't realize it?'

'Well, I was busy,' she blurted.

'Busy!!' spat the caretaker. 'You're not bloody busy. You've *never* been bloody busy. You're just bloody nosey. If you hadn't been such a bloody-minded cantankerous old cow, none of this would have happened.'

I thought first of all that Aggie was near to tears but she was made of sterner stuff. She began to fight back.

'Is this what I pay my rent for? To be insulted? Am I not entitled to a little service? Can't a decent woman make a mistake without being picked on by the likes of you?'

I thought this looked a good time to make my exit. Other than pride, nothing appeared to be too badly damaged. It

59

was council property and Aggie was a council tenant. I had a feeling that the discussion would go on for some time yet. I squeezed past the crowd of people in the living-room. They were even thicker in the passageway.

'What's the matter, guv?'

'What's going on in there?'

'Are they both dead?'

I gave a non-committal answer to each query.

As I left the exit from Nathan House and stepped out into the street, an elderly gentleman approached me.

'I came past here about half an hour ago on my way to draw my pension.' He paused. 'Well, I don't know if you're interested, but d'you know, I could swear I heard someone call out "HELP".'

It is the recurring problems that are the most insoluble for any home beat officer. That, doubtless, is why they recur in the first place. One of the most time-consuming aspects of community coppering is to officiate in the continuous war between the very young and the very old. This is almost always complicated by the design of many of the new housing estates. The interiors of the majority of these flats are usually excellent. The overall design, on the other hand, is frequently appalling. I often have the feeling that architects only became architects in the first place because they always disliked their grandparents. When one sees the location of many of these old people's houses, it is difficult to disprove this theory. Designers seem to be obsessed with the idea that old people love to hear the happy sound of children's voices. In reality, old people hate kids.

Clamps Court is a classic example. It is a small, intimate quadrangle of one-storey bed-sits. It has a couple of small lawns with a flowerbed in the centre, plus benches for the residents to rest on. The design of the building should have made the centre of the courtyard an enviable suntrap. Unfortunately, thirty seconds' walk to the east is a youth club. Forty seconds to the south is a junior school. Sixty seconds to the west, a mixed comprehensive. And, for good measure, a network of paths criss-cross the quadrangle. Here, kids on bikes and skates can zoom in between the elderly and infirm. Close on a thousand kids are daily milling about within a hundred yards of these flats. One does not have to be Christopher Wren to realize that there was a certain lack of overall planning.

On some occasions, old people can be as much of a problem as any child. While it is not uncommon to be requested by a parent to chastize verbally a wayward youngster, it is fairly unusual to have to chastize a wayward septuagenarian. If in these situations the kids are unpredictable, then the elderly can be far, far worse.

The Newington Old People's Home sits neatly in the middle of my home beat. It is a comparatively new building, neat in appearance and efficiently run. Many of the residents have had extremely hard existences and for the first time in their lives they are experiencing genuine care. There is no rigid discipline nor authoritarian attitudes in the home. On the other hand, it is essential that the residents live in harmony with each other, otherwise the system fails. The similarity between residents in the home and schoolchildren in a class can sometimes be astonishing. Small intrigues, petty jealousies and a little selfishness can manifest themselves in the residents' lounge, just as frequently as they do in the children's playground. A boy-meets-girl problem can be as common in the home as it is in the school. Finally, of course, in both institutions there is the occasional bully.

Max Twiner had been aggressive for most of his adult life. Small of stature, yet fiery of temper, he had found life in south London particularly difficult. After all, if you are going to pick on people with any regularity, it does not help if they are consistently bigger than you. Therefore, when

Max arrived in the Newington Home he thought he was in heaven.

Max had retained his health, most of his mobility and, unfortunately, all of his belligerence. The majority of the residents were older, weaker and frailer than he was and Max revelled in this fact. George Davey had lost a leg at Dunkirk, forty years earlier on his thirtieth birthday. He was as mild as Max was aggressive and it was soon noticeable to the staff that George's pocket money had always disappeared by Monday. Max never actually stole from George, he simply 'leaned' on him a little. As a result of this 'leaning', George felt obliged to provide Max with the odd luxury, such as cigarettes, the occasional bet and perhaps a drink. In a move to combat this, the staff decided to allocate George his pocket money daily, instead of weekly. The idea worked beautifully and Max was not at all happy.

The story was recounted to me by Ruth, the deputy matron of the home. 'He has not actually robbed him of the money,' she explained, 'but there is no doubt at all that Mr Davey is frightened of him. Is there any chance of your having a word with him? It may stop him before he becomes too out of hand.'

'Sure. Where is he now?'

'He's in his room.'

'And Mr Davey? I should like to see him first.'

'I've sent him out for a walk with Sarah, one of the older female residents. He should be back at any moment.' She glanced at her watch. 'It's now past tea-time and he's never late for a meal.'

'Okay, but when Mr Davey returns I'd like to see him as soon as possible. Without him, there's no evidence at all.'

'Certainly.'

Ruth then led me up the staircase to the first floor. As I followed her along the corridor (not a difficult task, Ruth being a very attractive woman!), I could see into many of the rooms. They were small, neat and very cosy, each furnished with a single bed. Arriving at the end of the corridor, she pointed to a partially opened door.

'He's in there. I'll leave you now and see you downstairs in my office when you have finished.'

'Okay – but don't forget Mr Davey.'

'I won't. I'll claim him just as soon as he returns.'

I knocked on the door.

'Yer?'

'I'd like to have a word with you, Mr Twiner. Can I come in?'

'Yer.'

I pushed open the door and walked in. He sat on the only chair in the room. I decided on an informal approach, so, removing my helmet, I sat on his bed. I ran over the whole situation as Ruth had explained it to me. I was careful to make no actual allegation. I just wanted him to realize that he could not hope to get away with anything like this again.

He listened to me quite patiently for about ten minutes, then, surprisingly, he said, 'Who are you?'

'Who am I? Well, why, I'm a policeman, of course. Who'd you think I am?'

'You are *not* a policeman,' he said, quietly but decisively.

'Don't be silly, of course I am!'

'No you are not.' He stood up and took a pace forward. 'I'm a policeman, and I'm seriously thinking of arresting you!'

I looked at him. Was he having me on? He did not seem as if he was. He looked like he believed everything that he was saying.

'Mr Twiner, will you listen to me please? I've come to talk to you because I am a policeman. Now –'

'I tell you, you are *not* a policeman!' he interrupted. 'I

am the only policeman here and if you don't go away I will go and get another policeman and we will arrest you.'

I searched my mind for proof. It seemed ridiculous. Here I was in full uniform and this blithering old idiot was disputing the fact that I was even in the force! I then said quite the silliest thing that I can ever recollect saying to anyone.

'I must be a policeman – look, I've got a helmet!'

'Right!' he exclaimed. 'That's it! I've had about enough of you. I'm going out now to find this other policeman and when I do, we're gonna come back and take you away!'

So saying, he marched quickly from the room and was halfway down the corridor before I could gather my wits. I had experienced all sorts of excuses and reactions since I had been in the force but never one like that. It left me totally speechless. I rose to my feet and retraced my path to the front office. As I passed the television room, I saw Max talking severely to himself. Ruth looked up and smiled sweetly as I entered her office.

'Everything go well?' she asked.

'No, it didn't!' I retorted. 'It went anything but well. I have never been so bewildered in my life. The old fool totally confused me.'

I recounted my interview to her.

'Oh yes,' she said, sympathetically. 'I should have told you about that. He often does things like that. Sometimes when the doctor examines him he claims he is a surgeon. He usually reckons he is going to get another surgeon with him and take off the doctor's leg.'

I sighed deeply. 'How about Mr Davey? Will he be all right? I mean, he won't wander off to fix the drains or something while I'm talking to him, will he?'

'Mr Davey', she said, 'is as good as gold. He is really a lovely innocent old chap; although I am now getting a little worried about him.' She looked again at her watch.

'They should have been back to tea thirty minutes ago. Talking about tea, would you like a cup?'

I gratefully accepted and while I was drinking it Ruth asked another member of the staff to see if Mr Davey had returned to his room. After a few minutes the girl returned. No, there was no sign of Mr Davey there.

'Then perhaps old Sarah's room?' suggested Ruth.

After all, they had gone for a stroll together. Perhaps she might know of his whereabouts. I was draining my second cup of tea when the girl returned to the office looking, I felt, somewhat flustered.

'Was Mr Davey there?' Ruth asked the girl.

'Er, yes, he is, and I think you'd better come quick!'

Ruth and I looked at each other anxiously as we both ran down the corridor that led to the rooms on the female side of the building. The girl reached the room fractionally before us. She pointed towards Sarah's bed. There, lying apparently asleep, was Sarah. On top of her was Ruth's 'lovely innocent old chap', alias George Davey.

'He can't get off!' exclaimed the girl.

'Well, he appeared to get on all right,' said Ruth, acidly.

'I haven't done anything, Miss, honest,' panted George.

'I hope you haven't – we're geriatric, not maternity. You'd better lie still and we'll lift you off.'

'All right, Miss,' whispered the grateful George.

During the 'lift-off' process, I could not but notice that the bedclothes had remained in place between both participants. George and Sarah were also still fully dressed. I pointed this out to Ruth.

'I was just seeing what it was like,' murmured George nostalgically.

Old Sarah's eyes were now wide open. She showed by her next question that she, at least, had kept her sense of priorities.

'We're not too late for tea, Ruth, are we?'

Ruth accompanied me to the front door and thanked me for my help.

'Well, I haven't done a thing, except help an old lady to have her tea at a respectable time. Besides, it was a lot more fun for old George than paying for Max's bets!'

Rewarding though such occasions are, there is one day that stands out above all others in the years that I spent on the Wharf Road manor. It was unequalled for relief and happiness. It was most truly a day of days. I had just forty-eight hours' warning of its arrival but I counted each second with the impatience of a five-year-old at Christmas. It was a milestone of happiness; an ascension day to tranquillity; a euphoric peak that made every other day an anti-climax. It was bliss, oh bliss – the day the O'Sheas moved house.

To describe Peggy O'Shea and her nine kids as a problem family would be the understatement of the age. They were more of a disaster area. They had been the biggest thorn in my side since my arrival on the home beat. The rows, the smells, the thieving and the disruption that originated from 54 Freeze House were unequalled anywhere on the Wharf Road manor. They were undoubtedly the closest knit family that I had ever known. They were happy, they were healthy, they were cunning, they were devious – and they were going! What would I do with my time? How would I fill the vacuum? I hugged myself with pleasure.

Their social worker had telephoned me at the station one superb Friday morning, to tell me the good news.

'They are moving out on Sunday at 9 a.m.,' he announced.

'They are actually *all* going, are they?' I asked, still not fully able to grasp my good fortune.

'That's correct,' he replied.

'That includes every single one of the kids?'

'Yes – well, that is, providing David doesn't get put away

66

this morning at juvenile court. He is due up for seven cases of theft from motor vehicles.'

David was thirteen years old and he had already been found guilty on fourteen previous occasions. Even Peggy could not have been very optimistic about his chances this time.

Friday morning was invariably court morning for the O'Sheas. Just as some people regularly set aside a couple of hours for shopping, so Peggy allowed Friday mornings for juvenile courts. With all of her kids under seventeen, there always seemed to be one, frequently two, who would be making a personal appearance before the bench. That Friday was no different. Peggy and all the family descended on the court to await the verdict. They were never any trouble. Peggy would sit quietly inside the court and the kids would wait patiently outside.

To say 'all the family' were at the court would not be strictly true. Twelve-year-old Peter had decided that as the flat would be vacant from two days hence, now would be an excellent time to remove the lead pipes from the water system. Now whatever gifts Peter may have been blessed with, plumbing was decidedly not one of them. Peter and water were not exactly compatible at the best of times. Now, with the flat flooding with the stuff, he decided that discretion was the better part of valour – and fled!

Around early afternoon I was called to Freeze House by neighbours who wondered why their linoleum was lifting and their ceiling tiles were falling. I was followed a few minutes later by Peggy. She stared for a moment at the cascade as it tumbled over the front doorstep. Then she turned to me and said softly, 'Well, Mr Cole, at least they won't be able to say we left it dirty.'

In all the trauma I had forgotten all about David's court appearance and I thought no more of him until Sunday morning. At 8.30 a.m. I made a point of being outside the

O'Sheas' for their impending departure. No local removal firm would undertake the task of moving the family, so the social worker had arranged for a local rag-and-bone merchant to convey them on his cart. As one by one the children climbed up on to the cart I noticed David. He had obviously not been sent away.

'David got off, then, Peggy?' I asked.

'Well, he was a bit lucky, Mr Cole. The "Old Goat" on the bench said to him, "You've got fourteen findings of guilt behind you and you are only thirteen. If you are not careful you are going to become a criminal." That wouldn't do, Mr Cole, would it?'

'It certainly wouldn't, Peggy,' I replied, with mock sincerity. 'So what did he get weighed off with in the end?'

'A two-pound fine, Mr Cole. I should think that'll teach him a lesson, wouldn't you?'

'I should think it would, Peggy, I should think it would.'

'Well, tat-ta, Mr Cole, it's been nice to know you, tat-ta.'

With that, she hoisted herself up alongside the pipe-smoking driver, and the horse slowly moved away.

'Goodbye, Peggy, and the best of luck,' I called. This time there was no false sincerity in my voice, just a great deal of relief.

Riot!

The urban riots of 1981 had no set pattern, at least as far as London was concerned. With the exception of the April disturbance at Brixton, which had complex and deep-rooted causes, most of them were begat out of opportunity or suggestion. There were nearly three months between that first single outbreak of violence and the country-wide pattern that was to follow. In between were the fairground disturbances at Finsbury Park, Peckham and Wanstead. But then fairground disturbances have been with us for some years now: candy floss and the big-dipper are out. The trend now is to attend two-hundred-strong and wreck the place. It is therefore misleading to refer to those months as a summer of rioting. There were, however, continuous rumours of riots and the general gut feeling that they were there, or just fractionally beneath the surface. This naturally had a considerable impact on the life of the ordinary street copper.

On Saturday, 11 April 1981, I had taken a day's annual leave in order to attend a wedding in the evening. During the afternoon, I began to hear reports of the early disturbances at Brixton as they came through on the radio. These reports, broadcast every few minutes on the many London radio stations, acted as a clarion call to people from all over the metropolis – and indeed from far outside it – either to watch or to take part. The result was that the number of potential rioters in the Brixton area swelled considerably.

Our early evening journey to the wedding took us through

Camberwell, some mile and a half from Brixton. The road from Camberwell to Brixton was closed and I saw many fire engines racing towards a distant red glow. There was an atmosphere and smell in the air that took me back instantly to the war days.

The wedding celebrations finished around midnight and we deliberately took a circular route home, well away from the troubled area. Switching on the radio, we discovered that the disturbances had shown no sign of abating. What I did *not* discover was that my telephone had rung almost incessantly from the time of our departure until just before our return. Every available able-bodied officer had been called back to their station. I was not due to report back for duty until 3 p.m. the next day; therefore, blissfully unaware, I slept well and had a leisurely Sunday-morning lie-in.

The condition and well-being of many of my colleagues during those twelve hours were, of course, totally different to mine. Take young 'Sparky' Harrison, for example. 'Sparky' is about as typical a young recruit as it is possible to find. He is a tall, slim, dark, curly-haired youth who sports an ever-so-slightly lost look: older women tend to want to mother him. He is someone who invites the old question: 'Why is it that when you get older, policemen look younger?' I remember being particularly impressed with him at a station disco. He has an incredible ability to move in six directions at once while dancing, a gift that he was to find extremely handy at Brixton.

Sparky had begun duty that Saturday at 7 a.m. Shortly before he was due to finish work at 3 p.m., he was asked if he would be prepared to stay on for a couple of hours' overtime. There was apparently a crowd beginning to mass in the Brixton area and a few PCs from each surrounding station were being asked to stay behind. Just as soon as the crowd dispersed, these additional coppers would be allowed to go home. Sparky volunteered: the overtime would be handy and he could still go out with his girlfriend in the evening. Just after 3 p.m., together with five of his Wharf Road colleagues, Sparky was driven the two short miles to Brixton by police van. Arriving at Brixton around 3.45 p.m., the contingent joined four other men from another station and the group, now ten in number, sat 'on reserve' in the police van in Railton Road. Railton Road is synonymous with all of the ills of Brixton. It is a seedy, run-down street that was referred to many times by both sides during the troubles as 'The Front Line'.

Eventually the men were split into pairs and sent out patrolling. Although this may have succeeded in placing policemen on the streets, it presented an additional problem caused by a scant local knowledge. Also, the vast increase of police in the area caused a grave shortage of personal radios. The sum total was that Sparky found himself in a hostile area that he did not know, with a colleague from another station whom he had never seen before, with no means of communication.

Around 5.30 p.m., the two officers turned into the western end of Effra Parade. The eastern end of this parade leads directly back into Railton Road. That particular junction was now littered with blazing cars. Police vehicles howled and klaxoned their way past the pair as they quickened their pace towards the scene of the disturbances. Neither Sparky nor his new colleague fully understood what had happened – or even what danger they were in. While they had been strolling around and trying to find their bearings, the whole situation had erupted in their absence.

As they finally turned the corner into Railton Road, a group of about two hundred black people who had been stoning the police further down the road suddenly turned

71

and saw the two young coppers. Realizing that the pair were now cut off from the rest of their colleagues, the mob charged towards them screaming, 'Kill them!!!'

Sparky then had his only real piece of luck of that day. A white motorist, who had been desperately trying to escape from the area, screeched to a halt. He threw open the passenger door of his car and the two coppers dived headlong into it. Amidst a hail of missiles and yells of frustration, the car then roared away with the two fugitives who could scarcely believe their good fortune. The driver of the car did a circular tour around the worst of the area and deposited both lads close to Brixton police station, thereby earning their undying gratitude. En route, they saw several police vehicles burning fiercely. Fire engines, rubble and glass were everywhere.

In an effort to stop a mob advancing on the police station, a chief inspector was attempting to muster enough men to form a barrier across the road. The intrepid pair joined them and faced the mob as the hail of missiles increased. By now, the first of the petrol bombs were making their appearances. Possibly even more sinister were the pieces of sharpened railings that were being thrown. These rusty objects had been cut to a suitable throwing length and then ground down to an almost razor-sharpness.

The problem of many police officers at that time was the basic shortage of equipment. Men had been drafted into the area from a whole variety of tasks around the metropolis. Some had neither cap nor helmet. The Metropolitan Police are issued with no weapons of offence, only defence. An eighteen-inch-long truncheon can hardly fend off petrol bombs and razored railings. In addition, there were several WPCs in the area. These young ladies do not even carry a truncheon, and as for their headgear – it is marginally inferior to the average tea-cosy.

By this time policemen were dropping everywhere, mainly

through head injuries. Many of the surviving members of the cordon pleaded with the fire brigade to help by turning their hosepipes on the crowd. This request was turned down on the grounds that it would not be allowed! To be fair to the brigade, they had enough problems of their own at that particular time.

Amidst all this turbulence, Sparky was aware of a bus travelling down the road towards the spot where he was standing. His first reaction was to wonder what sort of idiot bus driver would be driving in this area. His wonderment soon ceased when he saw petrol bombs being hurled from it. The vehicle had been hi-jacked and was being driven at the police lines, but the driver lost control and it crashed into a house near the cordon.

The rioters then used overturned cars to barricade off a section of streets and proceeded to loot every shop inside this cordon. The barriers had been strategically placed across the road adjacent to a demolition site. There was therefore no shortage of throwing material, and the cascade of missiles continued to pour unabated into the police ranks.

At this stage a rather brave, middle-aged black man appeared and asked the line of police if he could try to mediate with the rioters.

'Be my guest!' said the sergeant in charge of that particular section, only too pleased for a moment's respite.

The newcomer spread his arms wide and faced the mob.

'Dee-sperse! Dee-sperse! Law'n order at all times! Otherwise, these officers will be compelled to draw their guns!'

The renewed hail of bricks indicated that his pleas had been in vain. As if in consolation, a young PC quickly pulled out his pen and busied himself for about twenty seconds on a piece of paper. He then handed it to the man.

'Here y'are, mate!'

'What is it, officer?'

'I've drawn you a gun.'

The courageous newcomer joined with the coppers in their first laugh of the day. That was as close as the police got to using guns, although had rumour been true, scores of black people were being shot by the police, and the army was camped out on nearby Clapham Common, their tanks and armoured carriers ready to roll into Brixton at a moment's notice. This rumour caused a wry smile to appear on the faces of the smoke-blackened coppers who were still waiting for the plastic riot-shields to arrive.

A second moment of light relief happened when a motor-cyclist roared towards the police line, his registration plate covered, and hurled two petrol bombs. He then swerved and accelerated away, but just a little *too* fast because he lost control and fell off. Several policemen then broke ranks in order to capture him. He ran across a derelict site, the law in hot pursuit. His incentive must have been greater than theirs because he managed to escape. As the small group of coppers returned rather dejectedly to their colleagues, two of them made for the motor-cycle. Many of the mob who had not witnessed the incident somehow received the impression that it was a police machine. They fought off the two coppers, who in reality did not put up too much of a struggle, and demolished the bike, finally setting fire to it. Sometime later the rider was observed in a violent confrontation with several members of the mob! The coppers could not resist a moment of gloating.

It was now early evening and many of the injured police-men were being replaced by colleagues who had just finished duty at one of London's many football grounds. Around 7 p.m., Sparky saw his first protective shield of the day and he noticed that some police lines now had a further line of reserve behind them. Clearly visible to him by the light of the many fires were three masked figures in combat jackets. Sparky felt convinced that they possessed walkie-talkie radios because they appeared to be co-ordinating operations.

Some community leaders approached the police lines at this stage and held several meetings with senior police officers. Their view was that the police should withdraw altogether from the Brixton streets. The police, however, could not agree to this. They then crossed into the other side and conveyed to them the refusal of the police to do so. During one of these many pow-wows, a chief inspector, possibly suspecting treachery, took an escort of three police dogs, together with their handlers. These dogs were placed strategically behind him as he held his conversation in the centre of the darkened street. One of the dogs, a little more restless than the other two, came a little too close to the rear of the chief inspector. The animal then slowly, and without any great show of malice – he was, after all, a police-trained dog – sank his teeth into that gentleman's buttocks. To his eternal credit, the victim did not show his pain in any way other than to rise slowly up on the tip of his toes. The deputation from the other side was not even aware of the agony that their counterpart was going through. Nor were they aware of the excruciating embarrassment of the dog's handler, who was having visions of the sort of dialogue that he would be due for once the meeting had finished.

This blanket refusal of the police to leave the streets seemed to inflame the mob even more. 'It was bad enough up until that time, but after that, well, things just seemed to go berserk,' Sparky told me. 'Some of the crowd poured a liquid on the road and set fire to it. I don't know what it was but the fumes penetrated our lungs and made us cough violently. Shields caught fire, cars were set ablaze and pushed towards us. It went on for what seemed hours and hours. Snatch squads were formed but a different type of missile began to appear. These seemed to be like ammonia bombs; I could hardly breathe at times. The only light there was came from burning buildings and cars. Suddenly a petrol bomb crashed against my legs. I leapt back and looked *down* for the first time that night. I was then aware of a tremendous explosion in my head. The pain was unbearable. I came to for a few moments in the ambulance but I passed out again almost immediately. I woke up some time later in a hospital bed, not knowing where I was or what I was doing there. I apparently entered hospital at 10.10 p.m. I was discharged the following afternoon simply because there was insufficient room to keep me in there. [He had sustained a fracture of the skull and he was off duty for six weeks.] The bricks were easily explained, but as for the bottles – they must have been hoarding them for months, there seemed like millions of them.'

When I entered the station just before 3 p.m. the following day, I descended the stone staircase into the PCs' locker-room. While I was changing into my uniform, I was aware of some faltering footsteps coming down the same staircase. The feet seemed to negotiate two or three steps very quickly and then pause uncertainly for some seconds before tackling any more. Finally they clattered down the last two or three steps and Sparky appeared in the doorway. His uniform was absolutely filthy. There were scorch marks around his trouser legs and he carried the remains of his police helmet in his hand. It was literally in pieces. His face was ashen and unshaven. Blood had congealed on his tieless shirt and his eyes held a lost, glazed expression.

'What on earth has happened to you?'

He did not appear to know me at first.

'I – I got hurt at Brixton last night.'

'Where've you been till now?'

'Hospital, they've just released me.'

'But how did you get back?'

'Bus.'

'Bus! Like that?' I exclaimed, incredulously.

'There are so many blokes there that they can't possibly cope with them all. I'm going to report to the station officer, then I'm going to bed – for a year!'

He painfully removed his tunic and carefully placed the crumbling pieces of his helmet in his locker. I escorted him back up the stairs and eventually into the front office where I handed him over to the station officer. There the station officer recorded the details from Sparky's medical certificate and added his name to the ever-increasing sick-list. Sparky then left the building and became simply another statistic.

Well, Brixton had finally exploded. It had been promised for some time. Perhaps the only surprise was the ferocity of the explosion. For the first time for generations, society had discovered a fact which all policemen know almost as soon as they set foot in the streets: that the veneer around our civilization is paper-thin.

In the aftermath came the experts, from all over the country, even abroad. Politicians vied with each other to find explanations, yet succeeded only in throwing up a barrage of rhetoric. There was one who claimed that there were no rioters in Brixton – only 'freedom fighters'. Three of these 'freedom fighters' walked past Maurice's Hairdressers at 5.7 p.m. on that turbulent Saturday. There, PC Peter Strawbridge was standing guard over a broken window. They smashed his head with a brick and threw him in an unconscious state through the window, partially severing his foot.

The press also seemed to me to miss the point. One Sunday newspaper, for example, gave prominence to a photograph showing two plain-clothes police officers carrying what appeared to be pick-axe handles. 'How terrible' was the implication. Now many policemen who found themselves at Brixton on that day had to improvise in order to survive. They had been drafted in from all over the place. Many had no truncheons with them so had to pick up and use whatever they could to defend themselves. It was either that, or face the mob totally unarmed. Many of the young WPCs who were present did just that. This fact was not mentioned, even though it would have given the newspaper's article some balance. This photograph seemed to generate more excitement among some of the Sunday paper's readers than did the pillage that had taken place everywhere else. One reader from sleepy Blandford in deepest rural Dorset wrote to say that he felt the whole thing was 'deplorable and showed a complete lack of responsibility by the police'.

Well, perhaps he has a point. There is no doubt at all that through their confounded desire for survival the police prolong these disturbances. Perhaps instead they should form themselves into squares, minus their shields and truncheons. There they could be joined by the WPCs with their potentially lethal handbags. The mob could then pelt and burn them without interruption, getting the whole business over much more quickly.

It was on the second day at Brixton that a Xerox-copied directive was passed to all ranks. This sheet of paper did more for the morale of coppers in those hostile streets than anything else during that whole turbulent period. It was a directive composed by some anonymous officers and couched in the official police jargon which gave it a superbly authentic touch.

The following confidential instructions are to be brought to the attention of all ranks who are being supplied as 'Aid' to Commander of 'L'district [Brixton].

Dress: Trousers (pressed). Boots (shone). Reinforced helmets (brushed). Truncheons and whistles also to be carried.

Non-authorized Clothing: Crash helmets, steel-capped boots, jogging shoes and squad ties.

Inspectors in charge of each serial of men will search their officers at time of parade to ensure that no officers have concealed six-foot scaffold poles or pick-axe handles in their truncheon pockets.

Protective Clothing: The only protective item allowed is a police long-service and good-conduct medal. This must be worn in a prominent position so as to allow the local youth to identify old policemen, who they do not like, from young policemen, who they like even less.

The following practices have been noted and must cease forthwith. Missiles thrown at police should *not* be picked up and thrown back. Once these missiles have hit the ground they should be deemed 'Out of play'. However, missiles in mid-flight may be headed back, although prior to this helmets must be removed to prevent damage to the helmet plate.

The practice, especially amongst members of shield serials, of 'whooping like cowboys and Indians' and 'beating of truncheons on riot shields' must cease. This tends to frighten and intimidate rioters.

The practice of 'blacking up' faces is definitely inappropriate in the present conflict.

Sirens on police vehicles should not be used as these have been confused with air-raid warnings, causing an influx of residents into the underground station.

Members of the force must no longer abseil into Brixton Broadway from the roof of Woolworths, as the manager complains that this practice is damaging his burnt paintwork.

Officers who are set alight by petrol bombs should not run down the road screaming. They should lie down in the road with dignity and await their turn to be put out.

Officers attempting to obtain more than one permitted ham-roll will be dealt with severely by being returned to their own districts and not be allowed to attend future riots.

Before leaving for Brixton, inspectors should brief their men on local customs and traditions. It has been statistically proved that the young of the area are twenty times more helpful than youngsters in the rest of the country at carrying ladies' handbags. This action leads to something like two hundred misunderstandings per week.

Brixton, like the rest of the country, has its take-away shops. Only here the service includes jewellers, Burtons, Woolworths and camera shops. In fact it would be true to say that most shops in the area are in the take-away scheme.

The public houses are all 'free houses'.

The youngsters of the area hold celebrations similar to our 'Guy Fawkes Night' when pubs, shops and policemen are set alight.

Finally, should any elderly residents approach officers complaining of being assaulted or mugged, they should be closely questioned to ascertain if they are trying to start a riot.

The early, unofficial inquests into the causes of these riots put virtually all the blame on the police for their harassment of young black people over a very long period. There is no doubt that many young black people have been stopped by police. Almost all police/black confrontations begin over what is simply a routine piece of police work. I have helped at multi-racial youth clubs; I have taken black students into my home; I have taken problem black kids out for trips with my own family during school holidays; and I have appeared in uniform at the Old Bailey to speak up in defence of a sixteen-year-old black youth who had begun an affray that resulted in the death of a white teenager. Yet practically every time that I have spoken to a black youngster in the course of my police work, he or she will always reply: 'You're only stopping me because I'm black!' Twenty-five years ago, the question that a copper was most consistently asked was, 'What's the time?' Now it is, 'Why you harr-rass me, man?' This attitude presents an almost insuperable problem. The following incident is a classic example of how a policeman's intentions can be misunderstood.

My friend and colleague Jim Pierce heard on his personal radio that an eighty-four-year-old lady had been beaten to the ground by a mugger for the sum of £7 and a pension book. The description given was that of a black youth aged about fifteen, wearing a blue track-suit top, jeans and sneakers. This description was really no great help – that outfit is almost a statutory requirement for most black boys.

Jim was only two streets away from the incident but he decided not to go direct to the scene. Instead, he went immediately to a shop that has numerous gaming machines on display. These premises are havens for young muggers who, having robbed their victims, spend quickly and freely on the machines.

On entering the shop, he saw a boy who fitted the suspect's description in every detail. Taking the lad outside to the pavement, Jim questioned him about his recent movements. Time was the essence here: if this youth was not in fact the suspect, then Jim still needed sufficient time to renew his search. The lad himself did not seem too worried, answering every one of Jim's questions with a refreshing readiness. Suddenly a car screeched to a halt and a rather smart-looking black gentleman emerged. He introduced himself as a community worker and instantly stepped between Jim and the youth.

'Why are you questioning this boy?' he demanded.

Jim had by now satisfied himself that this lad was not the suspect. Ignoring the newcomer, Jim addressed his words to the youngster.

'Okay, son, off you go.'

The boy was just about to return to the machine premises when the community worker exclaimed, 'Wait!' He then turned to Jim and added, 'I want to know why you were questioning that boy!'

'I'm no longer questioning him. He fitted a description of a suspect but I'm quite satisfied that it is not him and he is now free to leave,' explained Jim, now anxiously realizing that the trail was becoming very cold.

'He cannot leave until he tells me what you asked him,' insisted the worker.

'Will you please get out of my way?' responded Jim, his voice now rising. 'I am trying to catch someone who has beaten and robbed an old lady and you are obstructing me!'

The community worker ignored Jim and took a hold on the youth. 'What did the officer ask you, and did he caution you?'

Not being too thrilled with either of the adults, the lad wriggled free and disappeared back into the shop.

The trail of the mugger was by that time so cold it was hardly worth pursuing. That comparatively small confrontation was not the end of the incident. There was still the victim – there is always the victim. What of her? At no time did the community worker mention her. Yet is she not part of the community? In fact victims seem, sadly, to occupy more and more of the community. It is a safe bet that she will never leave her front door for the rest of her life. Also, for every old lady who is mugged there are dozens of her neighbours who will now be too frightened to walk the streets. It is the victims who are locked inside – not the criminals. A £7 snatch can finish a life more effectively than any stroke. The resentment within the victim's own family is incalculable.

The initial unrest at Brixton slowly died down, although it did not totally disappear: it re-emerged in July some three months later. These new outbreaks were not so violent as those in April. This could have been because the police were better equipped, but more likely it was because the early riots had let off some of the steam. The police spent the first few weeks of this comparative calm licking their wounds. The many hundreds of officers who were injured gradually filtered back to duty. Two new words made their appearance in the everyday jargon of policing: 'low-profile' became the in-term. I cannot honestly claim that I have ever met a senior officer who has been able to define for me what low-profile really means. The consensus of opinion, certainly among the lower ranks, is that it means nothing, nothing at all. It means doing nothing, seeing nothing and saying nothing. At any briefing where the term low-profile was used, most PCs would simply turn themselves off. I have always assumed that low-profile is part of some great overall psychological plan. A plan which I am not mentally equipped to understand.

The early summer weather did not fulfil the role in the 'long hot summer' that the wiseacres had prophesied for us. The chill, sunless days were not compatible with rampaging through the streets, burning everything that could not be usefully stolen. However I suppose that sooner or later it had to come again and in early July rioting broke out in the Toxteth area of Liverpool. This spread first to Manchester and subsequently across the whole of the country. Maybe at that stage we should have had an agreed definition of exactly what constituted a 'riot': instead, the word was interpreted in its widest senses. On one 10.30 p.m. London area newsflash, a 'riot at Lewisham' actually consisted of two broken shop windows, an accomplishment that many Irish drunks would have considered to be well beneath their dignity.

These news items must surely have helped to spread the disturbances. One TV bulletin, for instance, showed a map of the country with little red throbbing spots where the latest outbreaks had been reported. It listed the towns that had experienced 'riots', reading them out like football results. 'Sheffield 3 – Leicester 4.' One could imagine an impressionable moron staring at the screen and realizing that his town had not had a mention. All he needed was four nights of rioting then his town could get into the first division. Next season they might even play Brixton! While it is impossible to prove it, my personal opinion is that the TV news bulletins could have only assisted the rioters more if they had provided them with transport.

On Friday, 10 July, after several sporadic outbreaks in places scattered around London, matters finally seemed about to come to a head. Together with six of my male colleagues and one female, I was on duty at a park at the rear of the Walworth Road where a two-day celebration of the twenty-fifth anniversary of the Duke of Edinburgh award scheme was to take place. There were to be numerous side-shows and stalls. Local schools, welfare day-centres, St John's ambulance brigade, police, fire brigade and ambulance service were all to exhibit their various skills. The highlight of the show was to be the Royal Marine display team. This would include abseiling, parachuting, a mock battle and an assault course. We had begun duty at 10 a.m. and were due to finish a short time after the show closed at 6 p.m. As the day wore on, tension in the area began to build and the stalls that featured the many local schools did not re-open after lunch. Spectators began to drift away early and by 4.30 p.m. the park was almost deserted. People anxiously plied us with questions.

'Where is the rioting going to be tonight?'

'I don't know,' I would answer. 'I didn't even know that we were going to have one.'

But nothing would placate them. I did not altogether blame them – there was so much rumour in the air. Just before 5 p.m. we were told by a message via our personal radios that we would not now be finishing at 6 p.m. It was more likely to be ten or even later. Violence had already broken out at Brixton and we heard the first of the emergency service vehicles as they threaded their way through the homeward-bound traffic.

Our group from the park had split into pairs and I was fortunate enough to be coupled with the only WPC in our party, the slim, attractive Jenny Hanks. We were both hoping to obtain a meal before starting our evening stint of overtime. On reaching the Walworth Road, we were astonished at the sight that met our eyes. Traffic was simply not moving: all the main roads were totally snarled up. The pavements were crowded with hordes of pedestrians, all of whom appeared to be scurrying along. Mums weighed down with heavy shopping bags doggedly tried to thread their way across the blocked roads. Men hastened along the pavements after their day's work, elbowing their way through the crowds in their determination to reach home.

Everywhere there was panic. It looked like the day before the end of the world. Shopkeepers and a multitude of handymen were busily engaged in boarding up the fronts of most shops. The colourful assortment of window displays had changed within a few hours to a drab array of tatty boards. Cowboy carpenters had made a real killing: £300 was being charged to board up the smallest of shop fronts. Some of the timber being used appeared anything but suitable. Most of it had the resilience of wet toilet tissue.

The journey from the park gates to Wharf Road police station would normally have taken Jenny and me five or six minutes. It took us no less than three-quarters of an hour. People formed queues to ask us questions. We were as bewildered as they were, although we never let on. We had come straight from the comparative tranquillity of the park to the siege state that was the Walworth Road. The vast majority of the questions were totally absurd, but people were genuinely frightened, of that there was no doubt at all.

'When is the march coming through?' they would ask.

'What march?' one of us would reply.

'Ten thousand National Front members are supposed to be marching along here soon.'

'I shouldn't think the National Front has ten thousand members. There is no march.'

'Yes there is! That's why the shopkeepers are boarding up! They've all been told that they are coming through here!'

'Who told them?'

'Everyone knows it! All the children were sent home from school because of it. They are marching everywhere, they are wrecking and burning everything.'

'You mean there are other marches?'

'Yes!!'

'Where?'

'Lewisham, Greenwich, Battersea, Brixton. They are all over London.'

What none of us knew was that the citizens of Lewisham, Greenwich, Battersea and Brixton were at that moment believing the pillaging was taking place in the Walworth Road. It was terror based on rumours spread by almost everyone. Among the worst culprits who spread rumours were some official bodies. Many children had indeed been released from school early. The district office of the Education Department had contacted many schools in the area to

86

ask if the big march had reached them yet. The Social Services called emergency meetings in the old people's homes to discuss the evacuation of the residents. A local youth officer assured me that five hundred black youths were battling with an equal number of National Front members at Lewisham. He compounded this by adding confidentially, 'I don't know why you don't leave the force now – you don't want all this aggravation at your age!' (I wondered fleetingly if I could get him boarded up.) The local council quickly evolved two distinct policies: (1) if it could move, drive it away; (2) if it could not be moved, board it up.

Rumour, counter-rumour, fantasies and dreams: all played their part. If someone was told a story then they added just a little more to it and passed it on to somebody else. More than five white teenagers walking together became a 'huge mob', and more than six black youths became 'hundreds'.

During the afternoon's displays in the park, the Royal Marine commandos had given an exhibition of abseiling from a helicopter. 'The army 'as been fetched in, Mr Cole, I've seen the 'elicopter.' The helicopter did indeed fly low over the area while it was lining up for the landing point. Clearly visible on its body at a height of 500 feet were the words 'Royal Navy'. No one who queued to ask us questions thought to query what the navy was doing in the Walworth Road. The only connection the area had ever had with the sea was the Grand Surrey Canal, and that had been drained twenty years previously.

If the youth leader had considered that I was too old for all of the aggravation, then there was no shortage of people telling Jenny that she was too young.

'They shouldn't 'ave young girls like 'er at times like this.'

Times like what?

If one took away the rumour and the terror, then it was in

fact quieter than normal for a Friday evening. A few cars were stolen – cars are always being stolen. An old lady had her handbag snatched, three kids went missing and there were a couple of fights in a local pub. All in all, a fairly mundane evening. (Unless, of course, you happened to be the old lady.) The rumours, however, continued unabated.

An hour or so later, suitably nourished with an ulcer-feeding fry-up, Jenny and I resumed a general patrol of the Walworth Road. Not that we could see very much in the shop windows. A great change, however, had come over the area. The commuters had finally filtered through our maze of back streets and the roads were strangely quiet. The vast majority of people, having reached home safely, were determined to stay there. Children were kept indoors and just a few hardy souls ventured along to their local pub. Small groups of older men, however, stood silently waiting on occasional street corners. When we spoke to them I could feel their embarrassment. They reminded me of camp followers. They had neither the ability, energy nor inclination to take an active role in anything that might develop, yet they would want to pretend, mainly to themselves, that they had been on the spot.

The overall picture of London that July evening had been one of *potential* unrest: only sporadic outbreaks of violence had actually taken place. Brixton had quietened appreciably, and, by and large, the city was calm. Whereas the early spring riots had been mainly anti-police, the recent trend had developed into pure looting expeditions. A large group would stampede down the High Street and break the windows of any shop whose goods they fancied. This was not political, this was primeval. It was an instinct as ancient as the cave-dwellers. It was simply a branch of the something-for-nothing syndrome.

All of us at Wharf Road felt that we had a human

element in our area who sooner or later would have to hit the Walworth Road shops. The problem was, when? It would be dark, of course, and sometime after the ten o'clock TV news on which they could see how the other 'teams' were progressing and gauge the competition. Those of us who had been on duty since ten o'clock that morning were not overpleased with this, but the 'High Noon' was due soon and we all sensed it.

Still the rumours continued to fly.

'Do you think that I should lock up and go to stay with my sister in Plymouth until this is all over?'

'No – why should you? Nothing has happened.'

'Oh, I don't know what to do. I think I'll go – I don't want to get burnt to death in my own flat.'

I assumed from this remark that she would be quite happy to die in someone else's.

'The milkman said that he hasn't seen a milk bottle on the estate for four days!'

'The milkman told you that?'

'Well, I believe that he told the woman on the top floor.'

'The National Front have hung three blacks from lamp-posts in Dalston!'

'There are NO lamp-posts in Dalston!!' (For all I knew, Dalston had the greatest collection of lamp-posts in the northern hemisphere, but the reply was effective.)

'Oh, well, perhaps he didn't say that then.'

'Who didn't say what?'

'My son – he's just come home from work.'

'Where does he work, for Christ's sake?'

'Well, actually he's out of work. But that's what they told him down the King's Arms.'

Around midnight the streets were quiet and deserted. The day-duty shifts, together with the recently arrived night-duty, intermingled in the canteen. Arrangements were being made to utilize a coach that would patrol the general area. Every effort was made to prevent those who had been on duty all day from having to do much more walking.

The coach finally left the station with about twenty-five PCs and two WPCs aboard. Further down the road in a side turning, was parked a police transit containing another dozen men. When the coach was about four hundred yards past the parked transit, someone casually looked back through the rear window. There, emerging from a side street, was the 'team'. About eighty figures came streaming out of the side street and immediately began to attack the windows of the main-road shops.

It was the best stroke of luck that law and order had had all day! The mob was exactly in between the two police vehicles and they were unaware of it. The personal radios back at Wharf Road chatted briskly but no further assistance was needed. The whole thing was over in a few minutes and the 'team' scattered in all directions. Prisoners were brought back to the station and the tension over the whole area seemed suddenly to ease. More importantly for Jenny and me, we were both now off duty!

That pleasant state was not to last for long, however, because we were due back at the station some seven hours later. This pattern of work-sleep-work carried on for days. At the end of that hectic month came the Royal Wedding. The whole of that summer seemed to have been one long round of work and overtime. The camaraderie, particularly among the lower ranks, was excellent but the wives suffered terribly. The long, endless hours, one somehow seemed to adjust to. Life became split into just two sections – work and home. Coppers, both men and women, would travel home briefly to recharge their sanity and return back to work a few hours later. My interest in everything else almost totally disappeared during this period. I am a keen cricket fan, yet I seemed never even to know the score in any of the Test matches. I simply forgot them. My garden was neglected and we stopped going to the theatre and cinema. Catering by the wives became almost impossible. Their questions when we telephoned them would always be the same: 'Are you all right?' 'What time will you be in?' 'What will you want to eat?' 'I don't know,' became the stereotype answer. Even women like my own wife Joan, who had experienced many years of this uncertainty, found it something of a strain. A few of the younger wives simply went straight home to mum.

Throughout these summer months, universal praise was heaped by police on their canteen staffs. They hardly ever failed us. If the police worked twenty hours at a stretch, then so did most of these ladies and gentlemen – the young and the old, the black and the white. Their family lives were as important to them as ours are to us, yet they were always there when we needed them. When they placed a big meal in front of me at five in the morning, I may not always have been able to eat it, but I sure as hell appreciated their efforts in putting it there.

During that July the disturbances gradually petered out. The exact reason for this was not clear. It was true that the Royal Wedding had begun to absorb much of the media's attention. As a result the television coverage of these inner-city disturbances had lessened. Perhaps, after all, there was no single reason for their decline. It may simply have been that they had run their natural course. The experts who had rushed to offer reasons for the original eruptions now offered equally unconvincing reasons for the comparative calm. Whatever the origins of these riots may have been, they certainly caused changes to be made. Whether attitudes have also changed remains to be seen. Anyway, what the hell is a riot? As one old copper said to me while queueing up for

91

food on the Royal Wedding day, 'Riots finished? Look, mate, in another fourteen days the football season starts – they have a riot every bloody week then!'

Sheffield 3 – Leicester 4 . . .

Easter 1981

The cold February sleet swirled down the Crescent as I sat curled up in my favourite armchair. I glanced through my diary with mild interest. Reading quickly through the April pages, I could hardly believe them. I double-checked; yes, it was true, right enough.

'Hey, guess what,' I called across to my wife Joan. 'For the first time in the twenty-nine years that I have been in the police force, I am weekly leave for the whole of the Easter period!'

My weekend leave for the month of April fell neatly across Good Friday, Saturday and Easter Sunday.

'Don't fancy doing any decorating, do you?' she asked, hopefully.

I pretended not to hear.

Policemen receive one weekend leave every four weeks and, with the constant changing of the Easter holiday dates, it had taken twenty-nine throws before I had finally hit a bull's-eye. Now I had managed a winner, I was determined to enjoy it. I ran quickly through the Easter possibilities. Sister-in-law in Dorset? Friends in Norfolk? Cinema? Football? Most certainly the parade of shire horses in Regent's Park. One thing was sure though – no decorating. Absolutely no decorating. Easter 1981 was going to be really good. It was going to be a preparation for all of those lovely free Easters I was going to experience when I leave the force in a year's time.

Seven days before Easter, the first stone was cast in the

Brixton riots. I had been in the force long enough to know exactly what that meant. There would be no country trips, no cinema and no shire horses. Football there still might be, although I would not be cheering on any team from an off-duty position on the terraces. In all probability, I would be on duty at the same game attempting to stop two morons from kicking each other's head in. The many Campaign for Nuclear Disarmament marches would, of course, be a change. Several marches were due to commence at points all over London. We had not had a CND march for over ten years now; it would be something of a reunion. The fairgrounds at Finsbury Park, Wanstead and Ealing would be places to avoid. The social requirements of attending holiday fairgrounds nowadays are to assemble 200-strong, then wreck the place and rob everyone.

The week that preceded Easter dragged by. My leave days had yet to be officially cancelled, although I had long given up any hope of them. At 11 p.m. on the Wednesday evening, the news was finally broken to me. I received a phone call from Alex Nash, a WPC at Wharf Road, who had the thankless task of phoning around and breaking the tidings to everyone.

'Hullo, Harry?' she cooed, brightly.

'Yes?' I answered, suspicious of anyone who rings up brightly at that time of night.

'Alex here. What would you like first, the good news or the bad?'

'Er –? Oh, the bad news, I suppose. It'll give me something to look forward to.'

'Well, you are on duty at six in the morning. You will do at least thirteen hours and all your weekly leaves are cancelled for an indefinite period.'

'Thanks-a-bunch. And the good news?'

'Sorry, H.,' she said sweetly, 'but there isn't any good news. I just told you that bit to cheer you up. 'Bye-eee.'

'What! Why you bloody –' The line was dead.

I'll say one thing for Alex. She knows the perfect moment to end a conversation.

In order for me to begin work at 6 a.m., I need to rise at about 4.30 a.m. For the first two hours of any working day, I am not one of the world's great conversationalists. I am, in fact, as my mother would more colourfully put it, 'like a bear with a sore head'. Being a community copper, I do not, as a general rule, parade for duty with the men and women on the more orthodox shifts. On entering the front office to book on duty that morning, I met three of my community colleagues. They had also received their call from Alex. Each of us was handed a detailed, typewritten directive concerning our local market. Almost the whole of the council team of market inspectors had been suspended the week before and, according to this memo, the market was now in grave danger of anarchy. Fly-pitchers and one-day traders were attempting to move in and the permanent stallholders were becoming incensed. These directions were explicitly detailed on one point: on no account were we to leave the market unless we were relieved by a member of the early-turn shift. A constant police presence was to be kept at all times throughout the day. It was, I suppose, understandable, with all our manpower commitments; the last thing we needed was a couple of warring factions arising in the market. I studied these instructions intently, being interrupted only at the end of my reading by Sergeant Peter Cage.

'I never thought I'd hear myself say it, Harry lad, but it's nice to see you! What are you doing this morning?'

'Don't you try to get around me, sergeant. I am on duty down the market for the whole day,' I answered, defensively.

'Well, I've got a few little jobs for you first,' he said, with a pleasant smile.

'Can't do 'em, sergeant, sorry and all that. We are not only down the market for the entire day but we are only to leave

95

it if we are relieved by a member of the early-turn. Orders from the chief superintendent.'

I wiggled the directions confidently under his nose. He studied them intently for a few minutes.

'I do see a problem there,' he murmured, thoughtfully.

'I don't! It's quite straightforward, look.' I ran a fingertip slowly and deliberately along the line: 'NOT-TO-LEAVE-UNLESS - RELIEVED - BY - A - MEMBER - OF - THE-EARLY-TURN. You'll never see anything much clearer than that, sergeant.'

He gave me a tolerant sort of look, then stroked his chin thoughtfully.

'Well, our problem is that we don't actually have an early-turn. They were 7 a.m. to 3 p.m. yesterday. When they finished here, they went straight over to Brixton at 3 p.m. and I haven't seen 'em since, although I understand they may be finishing there shortly. They will then have been on duty for twenty-four hours and I can't imagine any of them leaping from their beds in order to rush down the market to relieve you for your eggs and bacon.'

I groaned with self-pity. Of all the jobs around today, the market would have been the best. Giving a final glance at the memo from the chief superintendent, I slowly tore it up. The pieces I fluttered over Peter Cage's desk.

'Sergeant,' I sighed, 'you are a first-class pain-in-the-arse.'

'It's not the slightest use you flattering me, Constable Cole, I'm above that sort of thing.'

He could scarcely conceal a smile as he swept his meaty hands swiftly across the desk and deposited almost all of the pieces neatly into the wastebin.

'All right, all right. What've you got, then?' I wearily asked.

He glanced down his list.

'Well, let's see what you'd like. Hmmmm, two bail messages; a couple of burglaries; a family dispute (that's been going on and off since yesterday so it should be settling down nicely now); a burst water-main; three overnight prisoners to be conveyed to court. And oh yes! This here one is right up your street. Peckham Road – an injured cat.'

'I hate cats!'

'That's not what you told me. You are always going on about people who buy Japanese goods because you reckon the Japanese are killing all the cats.'

'Cats? Cats? That's not cats! That's bloody whales!'

'Whales, cats, what's the difference? All creatures great and small, you know.'

I took the list from his hand and made my customary mental note not to let Peter Cage wind me up so much in future. There is no question about it: I am a real challenge to him. If he can get me going – which he always does with ease – it simply makes his day. The infuriating thing is that I know this, yet I fall for it every time.

I put the calls in some sort of order and paused to decide whether to use my cycle. It would certainly have been convenient because most of my tasks seemed to be in opposite directions and the round trip looked about five miles. For some reason, a copper on a bike in London is guaranteed to cause passers-by to stare. I have even known people to call upon me to stop in order to take a photograph! Such is progress. The sleek £10,000, three-litre police car, with its highly trained crew, glides past almost unnoticed, yet PC Cole on his second-hand, ten-quid bike has his picture taken!

On reflection I decided to walk. Several of my allocated calls were in blocks of flats and it would have been extremely naïve to take a cycle there. Anyway, I was too conversant with the cycle-theft figures to take that sort of chance. Wouldn't Peter Cage have loved that? 'You've had your bike nicked, Constable Cole? Tut! Tut! We'd better call a policeman, then, hadn't we?' I was allocated seven pence per day for riding that cycle. I wouldn't have given Peter Cage that sort of glee for seven quid!

At 9.45 a.m., having completed most of the calls, I returned wearily to the station. I had found no trace of the cat. The three overnight prisoners had now to be escorted to Camberwell Court. This task is normally allocated to a 'prison bus' but, in keeping with everything else that weekend, it had broken down. It had been some years since I had escorted any prisoners to court, yet I was amazed how little they had changed. The three men looked the same prisoners I had seen throughout my whole police service. The first was Patrick Donovan, a slightly built, stubbly-chinned drunk. He shivered incessantly and produced from his pocket a tiny wisp of paper which had originally been the end of a very thin, hand-rolled cigarette.

'Hey-yer gotta light, Jimmy?' he croaked.

'You can't smoke in here,' interrupted the Station Officer, rather curtly. 'Put it back in your pocket and smoke it later.'

If he puts that back in his pocket, I thought, he'll never find it again.

It is a constant source of amazement to me, how drunks have this flair to produce cigarette ends. They manage it as naturally as other people breathe. No matter how thoroughly they are searched on arrest, as soon as they awake in the morning they'll produce a cigarette stub. The amount of clothing they wear bears no relation to the stubs they can conceal. I once saw a Glaswegian meths-drinker, clad only in odd shoes, a pocketless shirt and baggy trousers, produce something close to a dozen stubs, one after the other. This was four hours after being thoroughly searched. On the other hand, the reluctance of most PCs to plunge their hands into the deep, wet pockets of the average drunk doubtless assists this ability.

The second prisoner was David Debell, a smart, honest-faced, chatty young fellow of twenty-five. His face may have been honest but his hands certainly weren't. He had a mountain of previous convictions and was extremely well known to almost every Wharf Road copper. If any of them had seen him leaving a shop at two in the afternoon they would have been fairly suspicious – at two in the morning he had stood no chance!

Now no crook likes being arrested, but Dave seemed to mind it less than most. I quite liked him; that is, apart from his insistence on telling the most awful jokes. The fact that they were never very good jokes was not helped by his stutter, nor by his inability to remember the last line. He would falter his way through the most complicated story and invariably conclude by saying: 'No, w-w-wait a minute. I th-th-think I got th-th-that bit wr-wr-wrong!'

Dave had recently been released from prison and all the signs were that he was on his way back.

'M-m-morning, Mr Cole. Nice day, ain't it?'

'Will be, providing you don't tell me any of your jokes, Dave,' I churlishly replied.

'I'm o-o-off jokes today, Mr Cole. I've told him a f-f-few but he's a right miserable s-s-sod.' Dave pointed at the third member of the trio. 'I th-th-think he th-th-thinks he's a p-p-perlitikal p-p-prisoner!'

Sitting sullenly in the corner of the charge room was a stereotype of every rent-a-crowd protester that I had ever seen. He was a tall, slim man with badly worn jeans, a wrinkled leather jacket and fell-walking boots. His long, lank, fair hair was thinning rapidly and linked up with his strangely darkening beard. This seemed to leave just a small band of white flesh, high across his face. This band was in turn virtually hidden by an enormous pair of rimless, tinted spectacles. He sported an assortment of badges, half of which demanded that something or other be legalized and the remainder, that something else be banned. I glanced at the copy of the charge-sheet. Name: Paul DeWhitt. Age: 33 years. Occupation: Student. I had a bet with myself that his subject would be sociology. His offence was simply non-payment of a fine, incurred for an assault on a prostitute. Hardly a 'perlitikal' offence.

All three prisoners were then led out to the waiting van and within a few minutes were deposited at Camberwell Court. During those few minutes Patrick Donovan produced from his pockets no fewer than four cigarette stubs. The van driver lit the first for him and he chain-smoked the rest during the brief journey. Dave Debell hummed a couple of pop tunes rather well and Paul DeWhitt only glowered.

On our return to Wharf Road in the police van, I decided to use the opportunity to call in at one of the many take-away food shops en route, because the holiday weekend had effectively shut our station canteen. A few yards away from the shop-front a vagrant staggered, then urinated all over the pavement, while still fondly clutching an empty cider bottle. It seemed a sensible thing to leave my two colleagues plus the van driver to deal with him while I purchased their breakfasts. The shop had been open for only a few minutes, so, having collected their cash, I waved them away together with their prisoner and waited for the meals to be cooked.

Some thirty minutes later I entered the station mess-room and found all three officers expectantly waiting for their breakfasts to be served. I had negotiated 400 yards of the Walworth Road while clutching four chicken-and-chip boxes plus two cartons of beans, to receive nothing but abuse.

'What kept you?' demanded Stan Phillips impatiently, as he eagerly snatched his box.

'Chatting, I suppose,' chimed in Ben Lodge.

'I've never met anyone quite like you for talking to people. You're a professional gas-bag. I bet every meal you

100

ever buy is stone cold by the time you get it back to the nick.'

'*Everyone's* meal is going to be stone cold!' boomed Peter Cage, as he strode purposefully into the room.

'Who else was in the van with you and the prisoner, Ben?' he added.

'Just Stan and Tom Flynn the van driver, sarge,' replied Ben, puzzled.

'Are all three of you all right?' persisted Cage.

'Yes, why? Shouldn't we be?' A little anxiety had crept into Ben's tone.

'Well, your prisoner has more fleas than a thousand randy hedgehogs. If you were anywhere near him at all, I would suggest a little nit-picking would not come amiss.'

It was like the bears discovering Goldilocks. Three chairs rocketed back in unison as all three men rushed into the yard to remove their jackets.

Peter Cage then turned his attention to me.

'And where were you when this lousy drama was being played out?'

'Purchasing a much-needed meal, sergeant.'

'Well, those three will have to spend the next couple of hours at the council cleansing centre. What do they have in those little boxes?'

'Chicken, chips and beans, sergeant.'

'Have they paid for it?'

'Of course.'

'Well, there's no sense in letting it get cold, is there?' He raised his voice to a shout. 'Off to the council cleansing centre as fast as you can, lads. Oh – and take Dirty Dick with you.' A reference, no doubt, to their drunken companion.

The three heavily scratching policemen were now joined by a reluctant 'Dirty Dick'. They stampeded across the yard and into the blue police van. Two seconds later they roared out of the station gates and off down the Walworth Road.

'And don't forget to fumigate the van,' called Peter Cage, through a mouthful of Stan Phillips's chicken. He glanced over to me. 'It's a bit like the January sales,' he said, as he raised a greasy drumstick.

'How's that?' I queried, with only mild interest.

'Well, this shift started off on Monday with almost thirty men. Now here we are on Friday and all we've got left is you. I don't know if that makes you a rarity, or if it means that nobody wants you.'

Somehow we blundered through the day. The next few hours were fortunately quiet and the return of the freshly-scrubbed-and-baked brigade certainly eased our worries. All three men, plus Dirty Dick, certainly looked clean and re-freshed, but they still smelt to me like a recently scrubbed air-raid shelter.

At 7 p.m. we were relieved by the night duty. An hour later I eased myself into my armchair. There would just be time for a meal, then I would have to prepare for another twelve-hour shift on the following morning.

The alarm clock quickly raced around to 4.30 a.m. and soon I was sleepily driving down the Old Kent Road. In the distance a grey dawn was breaking over the docks. At 6 a.m. on any cloudy April morning in Southwark, the usual daily battle would be waged. One by one, the day would win the streets from the night, the dark chasms that lie between the tower-block flats being the last to fall.

The manpower situation for that Easter Saturday had marginally eased. The heavy policing of Brixton over the last few days had now been slightly relaxed. This, however, did not mean that I was free to return to my original task in the market. Oh no! Peter Cage had seen to that. He had accumulated numerous little jobs, again best suited for my own particular talents. The family dispute mentioned yesterday had now entered its third day. In addition, the burst water-main was still causing a problem. True, the actual pipe had now been repaired, but the resultant hole in the road was causing more traffic mayhem than the gushing waters had ever managed.

Finally, he concluded, 'There is a missing person from your patch. He left home on Good Friday and he hasn't been seen since.'

'What's his name?' I asked.

'Just a minute – I've got it here somewhere.' He rummaged amongst his papers for a few seconds then finally looked up. 'I can't seem to find it for the moment but if matey was wearing a long robe and sandals I wouldn't worry, he'll be back on Monday.'

Raising my eyes skywards, I took the papers from him and walked out on my beat. Later that morning I discovered that my missing person did not, of course, come from Nazareth. He did, however, come from Cyprus, and for Peter Cage that was close!

Another task on Peter's list related to an expected midday assembly at Camberwell Green. Here a group of anti-nuclear war protesters planned to assemble 250 demonstrators before marching off to somewhere near Crystal Palace. My job was simply to see them off. They were to be escorted en route by two transit-van loads of police. When by 1 p.m. only *three* people had arrived, the organizer, with some embarrassment, called the march off. This left one inspector, two sergeants, twenty constables, two transits, to say nothing of me on my bike, redundant. Another £1000 down the nuclear drain.

That Easter was unique. There were marches, meetings, demonstrations, football matches, charity races and fairgrounds. In addition, nearly two hundred policemen were still off duty, injured from the violence of the previous weekend. With most of the personnel at our station scattered at potential trouble-spots all over London, Wharf Road was very short of manpower indeed. This at least had the effect of making us very busy, and both the twelve-hour working days of Saturday and Sunday passed extremely quickly. Monday, on the other hand, would be completely different. It was my turn to join the reserve duty for many of these trouble-spots and I was bored to tears by the very thought of it.

At 2 p.m. on Easter Monday, thirty-six PCs, four WPCs, four sergeants and two inspectors waited patiently in the canteen at Wharf Road police station. The reason for our patient wait was that the coach allocated to convey us to our reserve position had failed to arrive. The pockets of most men bulged almost as much as the handbags of their female counterparts. It is incredible what some officers will take along on these occasions: biscuits, chocolate bars, sweets, newspapers, magazines, books, cigarettes, crib boards, playing cards, transistor radios, writing paper and even, for some sufferers, soft toilet paper (police station toilet rolls being notoriously bullet-proof). All these items can be found somewhere – in someone's pocket.

'All outside! The coach is here!' called an unpopular voice.

There is always some bloody idiot who cannot wait to tell you the bad news. Reluctantly the canteen emptied and a very long day indeed stretched ahead.

The transport used by police on these occasions is very much a question of the luck of the draw. Sometimes it is the small green twelve-seater police buses. These vehicles can best be likened to the Vietnamese prisoner-of-war tiger-cages. In the winter they freeze, in the summer they fry; they are harder than tungsten and agony for the haemorrhoids. On other occasions, rather plush, international coaches with sun roofs and stereos can be the surprise of the day. Thirdly, and most usual, is the type of coach that we found ourselves in that day. It was a forty-eight-seater, multi-coloured monster which had obviously been used for every transport job except horse-boxing. With a piano accordion on board, twenty crates of brown ale stowed on the luggage-racks and a destination like Brighton or Clacton, the old bus would have purred with nostalgia. For forty bored coppers on a chilly Easter Monday, though, the magic seemed sadly lacking.

Our first call was to a feeding centre just off the Old Kent Road. Here a large meal of braised steak, potatoes, carrots, roll and butter, Black Forest gateaux and coffee was served to us. This was exactly an hour and a half after I had finished a home-cooked meal of sausage-toad, chips and rhubarb crumble. I gave my meal to a colleague and settled for just a coffee – a gesture I was to regret as the hours dragged by. The meal itself seemed a far cry from the crowd policing of nearly thirty years ago. Then, no provision was made for food and the margarine that had run down my face on the state opening of Parliament had originated from the corned beef sandwich concealed under my helmet.

Suitably 'force-fed' and watered, the forty members of the Wharf Road constabulary were now considered fit for come what may.

In addition to the simmerings of Brixton, there were three large fairs held in London that day, at Ealing, Wanstead and Finsbury Park. These four locations are well scattered through the city; the reserve of police therefore needed to be somewhere central. Hence, no doubt, our arrival at a dere-lict railway goodsyard in Battersea. The word 'derelict' is synonymous with Battersea. The whole area is virtually one huge derelict site. The many riverside wharves, the countless railway sidings and the great factories and stoneyards, nearly all have fallen into decay or disuse.

Our driver steered the coach through the gateway of what appeared to be a comparatively small yard, but which turned out to be merely a corner of a long-abandoned freight depot. Twelve concrete platforms curved away west and into the distance. Parallel troughs still indicated where the railway lines had been. A roof of sorts still covered most of the platforms and everywhere were traces of undisturbed pigeons. To the north of the sidings and just beyond an area of rubble-strewn land lay a vast, gloomy, derelict riverside depository. This structure dominated the whole scene: it looked like the set of a cops-an'-robbers film.

Amidst the rubble, three neat lines of coaches and transits rested quietly with their doors fixed open. Around these vehicles, an assortment of games were being played – football, cricket, volley ball and rounders, plus bastardized versions of all these. Sweating, shirt-sleeved coppers kicked or belted an array of makeshift balls. Some WPCs joined in enthusiastically. While their football skills may not have been world class, some of their tackling was obviously fetching tears to the eyes. In the far distance – too far for the ball to be visible – six fellows and three girls were playing a game that looked to me suspiciously like kiss-chase. Of those who remained on the coaches, some read, a few wrote, but the majority simply slumped. The sun was now shining brightly but the north-east wind was biting. Cigarette smoke and stale air filled the rear of most vehicles, yet those sitting nearest the opened doors complained bitterly of the cold.

Our coach manoeuvred its way through the hills and holes and came to a halt behind the centre line of transport. Okay we're here, so what now?

'I've got a telly in case you'd like to see the snooker,' said our driver, quietly. 'I'm afraid it's only a small black-and-white set, though,' he added, apologetically.

Easter Monday was the final of the world snooker championship between Steve Davis and Cliff Thorburn and it was being screened on television. None of us had considered we would be fortunate enough to see it. This opportunity therefore would be a real bonus.

I had a seat halfway down the coach on the nearside. The driver now appeared to be advancing on me with a long cable in his hand.

'You'll 'ave ter lift yer feet up, mate,' he sang out, cheerily.

I looked down and saw, under my feet, a small trap-door. He pulled it back and exposed a pair of large batteries. As he bent down to fix the leads, I noticed for the first time the letters he sported on his sweat shirt: 'BILL FROM BILLERICAY' was emblazoned in fiery red capitals across his broad chest.

'You'll 'ave ter keep yer feet still, mate, or we might go up in flames,' he confided to me as he unrolled the lead towards the front of the coach.

He switched on the set and we all craned forward expectantly. Soon a commentator's voice was telling us of the super shot we had just missed. There then followed a few minutes of what appeared to be a driving arctic blizzard. This slowly evolved into an object with a large head and a long pole. By a series of bangs, adjustments, obscenities and tilts, we eventually made out a snooker table with two figures furtively flitting around it.

This was, as I have mentioned, a forty-eight-seater coach. The screen measured ten by eight inches and the picture was at best inconclusive, at worst indecipherable. In my opinion, all standard recruiting optical tests could now be abandoned. In their place should be a questionnaire which could relate to the balls on Billericay Bill's black-and-white magic lantern, as seen from the rear of his coach. As a snooker fan, I was confused beyond reason; but it was all we had and he did his best.

After two hours of this peering purgatory, a voice on the

tannoy system announced that 'serial 221 can now stand down for two hours'. We were serial '221', so this meant that we could now move beyond the immediate area of the coach. The four WPCs on board immediately rushed to the mobile toilets. (Why do WPCs *always* do that?) A few of us then decided to explore the yard in greater detail. A few minutes later, we climbed up to the second floor of the depository. A metallic sound of music and voices assailed our ears. Climbing the last of the stairs, we could see a patchwork wall of plywood and hardboard. Beyond this wall was clearly a cinema of sorts! Entering through a gap in the wall, I was amazed to discover some fifty coppers sitting in a makeshift auditorium. On the wall, with a clarity we'd almost forgotten, Goldie Hawn was deep in conversation with Dudley Moore.

Now the showing of films when a large number of men are on reserve for long periods is not unusual, although I personally rarely bother to watch them. For me, the drawbacks outweigh the amenity. First, I have never seen either the beginning or the end of any of these films. I always seem to arrive after they have started and leave before they finish. The acoustics are usually atrocious so great difficulty can be experienced with the dialogue. To make matters worse, this dialogue is always switched off for tannoy announcements. Should anyone enter or leave during the showing, then their shadow will obliterate a sizeable chunk of the screen. Finally, at the end of each reel the lights come on to enable the projectionist to rewind his spool – by hand. It has even been known for the right reel to appear in the wrong film. The renegade Indians who were attacking Charlton Heston experienced some difficulty slotting in on the underwater scene in *Poseidon Adventure*.

As a great fan of Goldie Hawn, I did feel morally obliged to stay and watch this film. I asked all around but no one seemed aware of its title. After a few minutes, a rather handsome detective appeared in the story. (Where do they actually go to in real life?) Goldie seemed very responsive and the whole thing was beginning to look quite promising. Suddenly the dialogue broke, a moment's pause, then, 'Serial 221 to their coach please.' I bloody knew it! It never fails! Every time I watch a film that happens!

Mutters and groans were the order of the day from the members of serial 221. Also from the rest of the audience whose view of Goldie was hidden by a group of moaning coppers. We hastened back to our coach to be greeted by the inspector.

'Sorry, lads, false alarm. They wanted five serial, urgently at Finsbury but we're on reserve for Brixton. I suggest you go for a cuppa. We'll be leaving soon anyway.'

Everyone streamed away towards the makeshift canteen except my colleague Jim Pierce and myself. We both decided to dash back upstairs to see how Goldie was doing, or, even better, how the detective was making out. As we came nearer, we could hear that the music was romantic and the voices soft. Jim and I looked hopefully at each other. On entering the gap in the wall, we saw Goldie dewy-eyed in a dressing-gown, with a rumpled bed in the background. Jim quickly turned his head to a young PC who sat staring adoringly at the screen. He opened his mouth to speak to the youngster. At that precise moment, the sound track was switched off in preparation for yet another tannoy announcement. Each copper present mentally prepared himself for his or her serial to be called. Ears were pricked and their attention was momentarily taken from the screen. Which serial would now be required to leave? We would know within seconds. A voice echoed all over the small auditorium. To my surprise, it was not the boring tone of the tannoy, nor was it the metallic tone of the film sound-track. No, it was Jim's voice, speaking in a stage whisper that must have been audible three streets away.

'Has he given her one yet?'

'Oh yes, Jim!' I said. 'Do let us get our priorities right. Ignore the acting. Disregard the direction. Never mind the sets. Forget about the script. All we have to concern ourselves with is – "Did he give her one?"'

I could almost see the review notices outside the cinema: 'Did Goldie get one?' – PC Jim Pierce. I looked for support from the smiling faces around us. I didn't get it. There was no doubt about it! He had given her one! Lucky sod!

'Serial 221 to the coaches please.'

I didn't care. I could never take that film seriously again, and we never did find out its title.

A few minutes later we were all settled in our coach and heading for Wiltshire Road, Brixton. Here we were to patrol the area in pairs until we were relieved. The 'pairs' policy had as much to do with geography as security. Probably three-quarters of our personnel had never even been to Brixton – and Brixton is a very easy place in which to become lost.

I was joined for this short trip by PC Alistair Leask, a work-mate of mine for some fifteen years. To my mind Alistair is truly unique; he has more airs and graces than anyone I know. Alistair simply radiates importance. It erupts from every pore. He should have been, at the very least, a Queen's Counsel, Field Marshal or First Sea Lord. Alistair had been making the rounds all afternoon, chatting to everyone in rotation. He considered he had a personal duty to do this. Now it was obviously my turn. I looked forward to our chat, for he never failed to entertain me. My opening remarks to Alistair were always the same.

'God, Alistair, but you are important! You must be the most important person I know.'

'Do you think so, dear boy? How nice of you to say so. Anyway, how are you?' I was about to say excruciatingly bored, when he interrupted. 'I say, can you smell burning?'

'Oh, it's those bloody smokers at the back,' I answered, pointing to the clouds of blue haze billowing along the coach.

'No, I don't think so, somehow,' he murmured. Raising his voice, he called up towards the front of the coach. 'I say! Driver, chappie! I do think that your coach may be on fire.'

Fortunately we had at that precise moment come to a standstill in Wiltshire Road. The driver spun round terror-stricken. I looked down at the trap-door under my feet. It was emitting a great deal of smoke! Alistair eased himself up and moved with great dignity towards the back of the coach.

Billericay Bill came hurtling down the gangway screaming: 'God we're on fire! Get out quick! QUICK!!'

I was about to do just that, when he suddenly hurled himself on me, yelling 'But don't panic!!'

Far from panicking, the whole coach erupted into gales of laughter.

He lifted the cover and found he had left in place the cable that had previously fed the television set. The whole thing had short-circuited; but, other than smoke and sparks, we appeared to be unscathed. Replacing the trap, Bill returned a little ruefully to the driver's seat. Over the police radio installed temporarily in the coach, we learned that the fairground at Finsbury Park was proving something of a jungle. Calls about robberies, assaults, criminal damage and arson streamed from the set. Many of the reserve coaches from our own base at Battersea were now arriving at Finsbury and slowly the terror diminished. Brixton, on the other hand, was as quiet as a grave.

For several hours we wandered aimlessly around the streets in pairs. I knew we would not be dismissed until Finsbury quietened, and slowly a very cold midnight passed. The emergency calls over the set slowly abated and somewhere around 3 a.m. came our dismissal. Billericay Bill turned the old coach around and headed back towards Wharf Road. Heads were still nodding as the coach came to a halt outside our own station. I looked across at Alistair; he even looked important when he was asleep!

At 4 a.m. I slid into bed; at quarter past eight the postman almost knocked in my front door with a parcel. It was a belated Easter egg for my daughter from a boyfriend. With great restraint I did not smash it over the postman's head. I took a cup of coffee back to bed and slowly took stock of the situation. I had just worked over sixty hours in five days. I was short of sleep and temper. I also had a book to write. I had not gone to Norfolk, Dorset, a football match, Regent's Park or the cinema, and it was supposed to have been my Easter off! Wild horses would not have dragged it from me, but I would much sooner have decorated.

'So you are trying to tell me that he went out of this car door and into Kingdom Come!' exclaimed Inspector Watts, making little attempt to hide his obvious disbelief.

'Well, er, yes, I suppose I am really,' replied Dewdrop Benskin.

Dewdrop, so-called because of the almost permanent droplet of moisture at the tip of his nose, did not sound very convincing.

'Well, then, tell me again, please, because I am just not grasping this at all,' insisted Watts.

Dewdrop sighed and was about to repeat yet again how it was that Georgie-boy Williams had met his untimely and violent death.

'No – wait!' interrupted Watts. He then turned his attention to me. 'Take Mr Harris out of earshot for the moment. I think it may assist Mr Benskin to remember all the important details if he is not overheard. When he has finished telling me, then perhaps Mr Harris may care to give us his version.'

The ashen-faced Harris said nothing, but watched Benskin's mouth intently, as if lip-reading every syllable.

The distant drone of Benskin's voice was soon drowned by the familiar noise of the approaching police van. A sound, I may add, that was almost as familiar to Harris as it was to me. Any nineteen-year-old lad with thirteen previous convictions inevitably acquires a certain, if limited, knowledge of police transport. The van swung smoothly around the corner and braked to a halt on the opposite side of Damson Street. PCs Steven Brown and Andrew McCluskey hurried forward and swiftly removed several 'road hazard' cones from within the van's interior. A minute or two later, a dozen cones, two metres apart, neatly circuited the silver-grey Ford Cortina saloon. Throughout this operation, the driver's door of the car had hung ominously open. Now, however, the forceful late-May breeze was gaining momentum and threatening to slam it shut. In an attempt to forestall this, Andrew McCluskey had stepped forward and wedged the last remaining cone between the sill and the bottom of the car door.

Suddenly aware of a restriction to his feet movements, Andrew glanced quickly down. Sergeant Cage's regular complaint about him came quickly to mind: 'The trouble with you, McCluskey, is that your brains are in your boots!' This, of course, was not true – there was simply no room for them there. All available space in those size twelve boots were taken up by those size thirteen feet. However, it was now fairly obvious, even to Andrew, that *someone*'s brains were down there and congealing fast on the road.

Georgie-boy Williams had never been very big on brains; the last thing he could have afforded was to have them spread over the road like marmalade. Then to have a bean-pole of a copper slush his insensitive way through them was probably the unkindest cut of all. At least it would have been unkind had Georgie-boy been in a position to care, but lying cold on some mortuary slab does tend to dispel trivia.

Poor Georgie had not been one of life's successes. His criminal career had begun at the age of thirteen, when together with his lifelong pal Dewdrop Benskin, he tip-toed into the local church and spent the next six hours removing the offertory box. If the contents of the box had been in ratio to the pair's expectations, they would have been able to retire, at least until they were sixteen.

The main problem for the couple was that the box was cemented into one of the stone pillars of the church. The scuffed knuckles and grazed wrists indicated their lack of expertise with both hammer and chisel. The sum contents of the box, 27½ pence, indicated their lack of any form of criminal intelligence. Their only consolation was their pride: they were convinced that they had pulled off the year's master-coup.

'Did a big screw-in last night,' murmured Georgie-boy off-handedly next day to a group of young admirers.

'Cor! Where, Georgie?'

'The Bishop's 'ouse.' ('Bishop's 'ouse' had somehow more status than St George's Church.) ''Ad a load of good gear from there, I can tell yer.'

''Ow much, Georgie?'

'Can't tell yer that – but enuff, all the same,' answered Georgie, with a knowing wink.

Georgie had thus entered the open university of small-time crime. Whether or not he graduated to the higher echelons of illegality would depend entirely on how much he learned from his experiences. Georgie had unfortunately learned nothing, and now he was dead. Poor Georgie.

'You understand you'll be expected to make a statement?' I heard Inspector Watts recite to Benskin.

'No, I didn't know that! I don't like making statements, not to you lot, anyway. You have a habit of making things up. Why 'ave I gotta make one?' protested Dewdrop.

'Because we have a dead body, that's why! We have one dead body and two live witnesses. That equals two big statements. If I understand you correctly, you are saying the dead man was hit by a car. I'm saying he looked more like

115

he'd been hit by the Albert Hall. I shall want a statement, not only from you but also from Harris. *And* I'll want them taken separately.'

'Well we didn't kill him,' whined Dewdrop.

'Convince me!' retorted Watts.

The reason for the inspector's disbelief was only too apparent. According to both witnesses, Williams had been driving the car and had stopped suddenly, saying that he believed one of his brake lights was not properly illuminated. He then allegedly slid out of the driver's door, leaving Harris in the front passenger seat and Benskin in the back. He had then begun his fateful walk to the rear of the vehicle, when a passing speeding car of unknown make, with an unseen number plate, sent him spinning six yards in the air. Being three-quarters decapitated and totally dead, Georgie-boy was at least spared the discomfort of Harris's first-aid. (Harris had always fancied himself as a first-aider. He saw himself as a sort of Mafia doctor.)

It was at this stage that the lads' stories became even more dubious. George Sidney Williams, Terence Anthony Benskin and Franklin Jonathon Harris had incurred fourteen, ten and thirteen previous convictions respectively. The total of their ages was still under sixty. Most of these crimes were for theft of, or from, motor vehicles. Just about the last reason in the world for which Georgie-boy would stop his car would be a suspicion that his brake light was not working correctly. In fact, as it was Georgie's own car, it was extremely unlikely that his brake lights had ever worked at all. (He had also acquired twenty-two traffic summonses.) While one would not wish to speak ill of the dead, it was an undeniable fact that Georgie Williams had probably committed more offences on the Queen's highway than had Dick Turpin.

When the police and ambulance crew had arrived at the scene, they were met by the sight of the body some few yards from the car. It lay crumpled on its side and very messy. The deceased had clearly sustained a really fearful blow to the head. Exactly what force had caused the blow, however, was not quite so clear. Soon Georgie-boy was bound and blanketed and slid smoothly into the rear of the ambulance.

'Where are you taking him?' asked Watts. 'Will it be St Thomas's casualty?'

'Too late for the casualty, mate,' replied the ambulance driver. 'Try the mortuary.'

Both Benskin and Harris were placed into the police van. They were then driven off to Wharf Road police station in order to make their statements, albeit reluctantly. Inspector Watts who, together with McCluskey, had been among the first policemen on the scene, also left for the station. McCluskey, however, called in at the mortuary on the way. Both officers would be required to view the body at the mortuary in order to provide a continuity of evidence of identification. This continuity was a recent requirement. It had been incorporated into standard practice only after the wrong body had arrived for a post-mortem! The reporting officer was now required to follow the body through all stages until the inquest.

It was now left to Stevie Brown and me to wait, first for the official police photographer, then for the removal vehicle which would tow away the Ford to the police station. Some thirty minutes later, another Ford, this time a rusty, twenty-year-old Pilot saloon, coughed and spluttered its way along Damson Street. Ship-like, it steered a slow path round the traffic cones, finally docking at the kerbside. A very familiar figure alighted.

Sidney Eric Williams was an absolute 'throw-back'. His whole appearance was preserved in its 1945 state. During that period, Sid had been commonly referred to as a 'spiv'. A spiv could earn his living on either side of the law. He would dress usually in a small trilby hat and a long overcoat –

mainly black, although the more successful spivs wore fawn or brown. His suit would be dark and boldly striped, as would his shirt. His tie would be wide and hand-painted, his patent-leather shoes, shiny and pointed. A neat pencil-line moustache would round off the image. A spiv could always sell you anything that was in really short supply. His merchandise would range from a tin of corned beef to a cup-final ticket. In any negotiations, he would always look furtively right and left before speaking to you. This action implied that he treated you with the greatest confidence and you would be privileged and wise to purchase whatever goods he was offering. Indeed, you were not simply being offered a bargain, you were being offered an act of trust.

Sidney had never forgotten those halcyon days just after the last war. For him, life had been sweet and the pickings had been marvellous. Sid's one trouble was, he had been expecting them back ever since; in fact he still dressed for them. This was not only unfortunate but also possibly the greatest chink in Sid's armour. Fifty-two-year-old spivs somehow seem to lack charisma. His tycoon image was further dented by his persevering with his ancient car. The constant stream of smoke from its exhaust convinced many pedestrians that it ran on damp wood.

Sid was also an opinionist. The only mistake he ever admitted making during his adult life concerned a family friend, one Betty Copeland. In a rash moment after a cousin's wedding party, Sid, much to his astonishment, managed to put Betty in the family way. Betty was in fact a blow to Sid's pride. She was a skinny bean-pole of a girl who had only excited Sid's passion on that one regrettable occasion. A wedding was quickly arranged and a few months later the bride walked happily down the aisle, proudly sporting the first genuine curve of her life. Four months later, little George Sidney began his comparatively short stay.

It had taken ten months for Betty finally to return home to mum, taking little Georgie-boy with her. Sid had never been cut out for matrimony so the arrangement suited him well. The idea of providing for his family had never entered his head. He considered Betty, with her complaining ways, no great loss. The fact that she had taken his son and heir with her was an additional bonus. His view changed, however, once the child showed his father's flair for being light-fingered and devious. A son to be proud of, one might say.

Sid now leapt quickly from the car, pausing only to adjust his greasy hat.

'Now,' he said, matter-of-factly, as if discussing the opening offer for a nicked box of nylons, 'I understand you've killed my boy.'

'What?' I answered unbelievingly.

'My boy. My Georgie-boy. I hear that the law have done him in. I think I could have a good claim against you lot.'

'Well, you hear wrong. Georgie is most certainly dead, as you seem to be aware, but we didn't kill him! It seems he was struck by a hit-and-run car. Are you claiming that it was a police car that hit him?'

'Car?' retorted Sid. 'Weren't no bloody car! He was hit by a bloody great whee ...' Suddenly he stopped talking; he seemed barely to move his head, yet his eyes surveyed the whole scene: the car, the blood, the road and the cones. 'Oh – er,' he faltered. 'You've had an accident here, then, have you? Oh, all right, I'll leave you alone then. I suppose you must be busy. I'll be getting along.'

Without more ado, he returned smartly to his car. After the customary splutters, backfires and smoke, the vehicle jerked uncertainly away, gradually gathering momentum like a boulder down a hill.

Stevie Brown and I were in something of a dilemma. It seemed that Sid knew a great deal more than we did. We could perhaps have detained him; on the other hand, Sid was never too difficult to find. In any case, we could not leave the scene before the photographer and the towing unit arrived. If we did, the gawping ghouls who were even now assembling on the pavement opposite would have a field day.

'You know, I think he was about to say that the boy was killed by a wheel,' said Steve, thoughtfully. 'And the impression I received from that, was that this wheel was something much larger than, or different from your average car-wheel.' He paused for a moment, then continued, 'There's McGinley's building site in the next street. Perhaps there's an earth-remover or something very similar in use there.'

'I don't see the point,' I said. 'No one gets knocked down by an earth-remover, but even if anyone did, why make up a cock-and-bull story about being killed by a hit-and-run driver in Damson Street? Wouldn't it be much simpler to tell the truth – assuming that that pair could ever tell the truth.'

'Look,' explained Steve, 'suppose they were actually in the building site to commit some villainy, okay? Then just suppose Georgie-boy was somehow killed in there. The two survivors would be in all sorts of trouble with the law, agreed?'

I nodded.

'All right, so they carried the body from the site and into the next street. In this way they could claim that Georgie had been walloped anonymously, and finally, by a bigger villain than he was himself. In this way they are just the innocent victims of circumstance.'

'But it was soon after six in the evening! Someone surely must have seen them?'

120

'Not necessarily. The building site closes at 5 p.m. Both streets are derelict and they did not have to travel far. It was a calculated risk and they took it. They are two very experienced kids, you know.'

I had to agree with that last observation, although I still had doubts about Steve's basic theory.

'Well, how does old man Williams fit into the story?' I asked. 'And how come he arrives at this place and not at the building site? And while you are explaining that, how come he thinks we killed his boy?'

There was a long silence, I could almost hear Steve's brain turning over.

'This street is on the direct route from Sid's flat to McGinley's site, yes?'

'Yes.'

'Sid did not at first realize that it was Georgie's accident that we were dealing with. He didn't ask to see the body; he asked nothing about the car or if anyone else was involved. Sid was on his way somewhere else. It was at that "some-where else" that he expected to see the dead Georgie. The fact that he arrived here first was pure coincidence.'

'Yes, but that still does not explain why he thought we killed him!'

'I bet you that when we arrive at the site we'll find out exactly what happened. Then we'll know why old man Williams thinks we did in his boy.'

'It could be the lads were telling the truth, you know,' I murmured unconvincingly.

'Bloody hell, but you're gullible!' exploded Steve. 'I tell you what, you wait here for the photographer and towing unit and I'll go to McGinley's. It'll be dark in an hour; if we don't go soon, we won't be able to see anything at all.'

'You're enjoying this, aren't you?' I said.

'Yes, I think it's fascinating. Why – don't you?'

'I may do after we get this road hosed down. There's still

121

quite a bit of Georgie-boy lying around here, you know.'

Steve could not hide his impatience as he quickly disappeared around the corner in the direction of McGinley's. It was now 8 p.m., the time when both of us were due to go off duty. If Steve found nothing at the site then we would be away very soon. If, on the other hand, there *was* something there, well, then it had all the makings of a very long night indeed.

Some ten minutes later the photographer arrived in a small van. He took a dozen or so photographs from an assortment of angles and was soon gone. His departure was immediately followed by the arrival of a huge navy-blue lorry with an in-built hoist. I removed the traffic cones to enable the great vehicle to manoeuvre into a position parallel to the car. Two giant steel arms then projected out and easily deposited the car on to the broad back of the lorry. A polite request to the fire brigade to hose away the last remaining traces of Georgie-boy and I was soon hot-footing it down to McGinley's.

I was admitted to the site by the unit security guard. He was a servile, Uriah Heepish sort of individual who reeked permanently of drink. He wore an ill-fitting navy-blue uniform with a cap about three sizes too large.

'Your colleague is on the far corner of the site, sir. He told me you were coming, so I waited at the gate, sir. If there's anything you'd like me to do, just let me know, sir, I'll be in my office, sir.'

He made me feel too uncomfortable to hold any form of conversation. I nodded my thanks as politely as I could and scurried away between the cement mixers.

'Steve!' I exclaimed facetiously. 'No one, but no one, has ever been knocked down by a hit-and-run cement mixer!'

'I just can't understand it,' said Steve, dejectedly. 'There are three dumper truckers, two lorries and a tractor on this site. I've examined the wheels of each of them and there's absolutely nothing to show for it. Just dried cement and mud, not a trace of blood anywhere.'

'Look, Steve, this may not even be the correct site. After all, there are several other building sites in the area and it could be any of them, *if* in fact he died on a site at all.'

'That kid was killed instantly. He didn't walk anywhere, he didn't crawl anywhere, he had to be carried, and those lying little bastards couldn't have carried him far, not at 6.30 in the evening. This simply has to be the place.'

'Well, it's practically dark. What you say we have a final word with the security guard, then return to the nick? Perhaps something has come to light there?'

'One last look, then,' answered Steve, doggedly, as he strode off into yet another dark corner.

The daylight was now fast fading as we peered as best we could into the many recesses of the site. A sudden oath from Steve made me think he had found something, but it turned out that he had simply fallen over a builder's capsized wheelbarrow. Rubbing his shins vigorously, he finally agreed to the futility of further search.

Uriah Heep sat in his cabin drooling over an old Sunday newspaper. 'My wild love night with a rock star,' screamed the headline. He was more unsavoury in those close confines than he had ever been in the open air.

'Have another think,' said Steve. 'Did you see anyone at all hanging around the site once the staff had left?'

'No, sir. No one at all, sir. If there'd been anyone at all, sir, I'd'a' seen 'em, sir.' He paused. 'I'm nothing if I'm not thorough, sir,' he added, with an unusual air of confidence.

'Well, if you think of anything later, let me know. You can always contact me at Wharf Road police station. All right?'

'Yes, sir.'

I was beginning to find Steve's attitude quite amusing. He was slowly convincing himself that this was a big murder job. Another hour and the Interpol phones would be ringing all over Europe.

'You'd better let Inspector Watts in on the act, not to mention the CID,' I whispered, as we strolled out into the dark.

'Yes, er, well, he can contact them through me.'

'One more thing, Steve.'

'Yeh?'

'Don't be so bloody pompous.'

Some fifteen minutes later we climbed the front steps of the station. Watts and Andrew McCluskey had made their formal identification of the body and were now engaged in the taking of statements. There were numerous routine enquiries to be made, most of which the inspector had already set in motion. Stevie Brown had suitably busied himself at the scene and at the building site and I felt superfluous. I decided it was time to go home.

I called in at the interview room and spoke to Watts, who was hardly ecstatic at the interruption.

'I should have been off duty an hour ago, guv. If you've nothing else for me to do, I'll hop it.'

He nodded and waved me irritably away.

It is on occasions such as this that I wonder if I was wise in becoming a policeman. I hate puzzles, basically because I am useless at them. I really envied Stevie Brown his dedication. In the main, I believe what people tell me; if they lie, I become confused. I found this whole case really a bore. Why couldn't it be a nice, straightforward accident or an equally straightforward murder? I wanted tomorrow to come quickly and perhaps then someone – certainly not me – would have solved the mystery.

Glancing at my watch, I decided to call in at the Duke of Sutherland. Two pints of best bitter tends to lift my despondency. The pub is situated just off the Walworth Road and is an equal distance between the station and the scene of the fatal accident. I sat at the bar and exchanged pleasantries with Tom, the landlord. Suddenly our conversation was interrupted by Albert, a retired market porter.

''Ere, 'Addy.' (God knows why, but he always pronounced my name in that manner.) 'Can't you do somefink abaht them bleedin' kids in the square?'

'What kids?' I asked tersely, really resenting this off-duty interruption.

'Them bleedin' kids on the swing, 'Addy. They're soddin' abaht aht there till nigh on one in the mornin' some nights, 'Addy.'

Actually I knew only too well 'what kids'. A nursery playground had been situated in a nearby square, with several tall trees around its perimeter and overhanging the road. The nursery had been vandalized so many times that the staff had given up the fight and the place closed. The vandalism then increased tenfold. Finally, after the fourth or fifth fire, it was practically razed to the ground. Ropes had then mysteriously appeared. They hung from the highest branches of these surrounding trees and youngsters used them as an enormous swing. The leaping-off point for this swing was a brick wall twelve feet in height and adjacent to one of the trees. The momentum of the swing, plus its height, would carry each of the swingers on an arc that spanned the width of the road. The pendulum would then reach its full extent some twenty feet above the opposite pavement.

As the local copper, this swing posed me with a problem. The swing was very high, it was unsupervised, and it had no safety measures. Underneath the ropes were a few railings, some steps, a brick wall and a road! Fortunately, few vehicles used the square, but those that did could well be subjected to 'buzzing'. This would entail one, sometimes two, of the more daring lads, flashing across the bonnet of a car and cheering their heads off. The swing was used by children of all ages between six and eighteen. The younger ones would arrive direct from school, the older ones taking over later in the evening. At holidays and weekends the swing was in constant use from early morning until late at night. It was by no means unusual to see as many as twenty children playing around its base. This was often a higher number of kids than were present in the nearby youth club. Almost regardless of weather, the swing would be in use. Radios would be played, cycles ridden, romances started. For some three years, that swing was a focal point for a very great number of children in the neighbourhood.

Undoubtedly a great deal of annoyance was caused to nearby residents, yet Albert's complaint was only the third one I had received in those three years. My dilemma was that the kids were actually doing something that they themselves wished to do and had originated themselves. Another point in favour of the swing, was its incredible accident-free record. It should have had three fatals per week – but somehow it didn't. Cuts and bruises, and friction burns to hands, bums and knickers, all were cheerfully tolerated.

Returning my empty glass to the counter, I sorrowfully refused Albert's 'one for the road' offer and made my first move for home. I decided to go via the square. Few of the kids recognized my car and it would be interesting to see if I sustained a 'buzzing'. Driving under the tall trees, I saw just a handful of kids sitting forlornly on the pavement. Of the swing there was no sign. I stopped the car and wound down the window.

'No swing tonight, lads?'

'Nah, PC Cole, it's broke, ennit?'

This had never before been a problem. Whenever a swing had broken previously, a replacement had always arrived within twenty-four hours. This had, of course, been a constant puzzle to me, but I had searched our crime books thoroughly and no such loss had ever been reported. I had also made numerous local enquiries. After one rumour that the ropes had been removed from the nearby fire station, I had even called on the brigade. They showed great interest in the quality of the ropes, but, apart from envy, contributed nothing. Now, for the first time in three years, the square was swingless. I never thought I would have admitted it, but it somehow looked empty.

'Is it true that Georgie-boy's dead, PC Cole?' asked a freckly-nosed kid of about twelve.

'Yes, I'm afraid it is.'

''Ow was 'e killed, then?'

'Well, at the moment it looks like he was killed by a car that failed to stop.'

All five boys looked at one another, then visibly brightened.

'Oh, that's all right, then,' said Freckles.

'What d'you mean, all right?' I asked, suspiciously.

'Well, we 'eard 'e'd 'ad a norrible accident.'

'Well, isn't being knocked down and killed by a car that failed to stop a "norrible accident"?'

'Well, yeh, I s'pose it is really – it's just that we 'eard that Georgie was murdered or somethin' like that.'

'Who said so?'

'*All* the kids are saying so, PC Cole.'

Now while this observation in itself may have sounded suspicious, I had to take into account that rumour runs rife on the Wharf Road manor. Not only would the rumour be rife but every kid would add the fantasy of his own imagination to it. By tomorrow morning, Georgie would probably have been killed by Concorde while legging it across the Heathrow runway. Georgie and the two survivors of the 'accident' had been three of the older kids who had frequented the swing. I therefore offered my condolences to the five little mourners and drove home.

*

127

For the rest of the evening I thought very little about the day's happenings. Stevie Brown, on the other hand, had thought of little else except Georgie's death. He had returned yet again to the building site but had been unable to gain access. The security guard, meanwhile, was making yet another of his frequent trips to a nearby pub.

The interview room at Wharf Road was purely a make-shift structure. The walls had been placed around a small section of the old snooker room. The result was a very small room with a very high ceiling. The acoustics were something akin to those you might expect if conversing in a dustbin. Inspector Watts's resonant voice vibrated into every corner.

'I've read your statement, Mr Benskin, and there's just a couple of points about which I'm not too happy. The actual injuries to the dead man's head could only have been inflicted by a car travelling at a very high speed. We agree on that?'

'Yes,' murmured Benskin, suspiciously.

'Yet my traffic patrol officers tell me that if a car sustained that sort of an impact, then there should have been debris in the road.'

'What's "debris"?' asked the young man.

'Dried mud from under the wheel arches. You and Harris both agree that Williams was struck by the front nearside wing of the car?'

Benskin nodded.

'Well all right, in that case I want debris – and you haven't given me any. There's one other thing that you'd better think about as well.' Watts now looked straight into Benskin's eyes. 'The pathologist will examine that wound thoroughly and if he doesn't find any car paint in it ...' He left the sentence unfinished but there was no doubt at all of its meaning.

'How – how can he tell if there's car paint? It wouldn't show, would it?' Terry Benskin was beginning to sound very cornered.

'He'd tell by using a microscope. If there's paint, he'll find it. If there's anything else, he'll find that too.'

'Anyfing else?'

'Yes, if Georgie was struck by some other object, then it would have left a trace. It's that "trace" which will tell me if you've been telling me the truth.'

Terry was silent for a moment. 'I'm not saying he was, mind you, but supposin' –' his voice faltered and faded momentarily. 'Just supposin' that Georgie-boy was accidentally killed somewhere else. Supposin' that we, well, we made a sorta mistake.'

'What sort of mistake? Would it be the sort of mistake that removes a dead body from one place to another? Would it be that sort of mistake?'

Terry did not answer.

'Well, would it?' insisted the inspector.

'Well, yeh. I suppose that it would be.'

'Well, in that case I'll get another form. I'm sure you would now like to make a whole new statement, wouldn't you?'

'I fink I'd better,' agreed Terry, dejectedly.

Frankie Harris was then acquainted with the fact that his statement now had more holes than a net curtain. Frank looked angrily towards Benskin but soon changed his attitude. Both lads then almost competed to tell the truth.

All three boys had been on the swing late on the previous evening. They had clung on to the rope and attempted to knock over a passing skateboarder. The skateboarder had ducked, the rope had broken and the three lads had fallen into a heap in the road. Their injuries were negligible but they were now under a great deal of pressure to replace the rope. The ropes were usually replaced in rotation from local building sites. (Ah-ha!) No rope had been stolen from McGinley's for over two months, so they were well due a visit. (When asked why the ropes were removed solely from building sites, both boys agreed that so much gear is stolen from these sites that no one ever notices a rope!)

Their visit was planned for 5.30 p.m. This time was deliberately chosen as being after the staff had left for home and before the security guard arrived. The guard in fact arrived at 4.30 p.m. but always slipped away in time for the pubs to open at 5.30 p.m. The three boys believed, therefore, that he did not arrive at the site until 6.30 p.m. In the centre of the site was a partially completed structure some three storeys high. A rope pulley hung down invitingly with a large builder's basket attached to one end. Frankie Harris climbed the ladders to the top and began to unhook the rope from the pulley. Georgie-boy meanwhile busied himself at the bottom by calling out instructions, and Terry appointed himself lookout.

On the top floor of the structure, near the edge of the scaffold, stood an old iron wheelbarrow. It contained a large heap of broken bricks. The position of this barrow seriously interfered with Frank's attempts to unhook the rope from the pulley.

'Move the bloody thing, Frank!' called Georgie impatiently.

'It's too sodding heavy!' grunted Frank, as he wrestled with the rusty handles.

'Well, tip it over – then bloody move it!'

Terry, who was easily the most nervous of the three boys, was fast becoming uneasy. The sight of silver buttons on a blue uniform approaching the side gate did nothing to help his mental state.

'Copper!!' he screamed.

Georgie-boy ceased advising the sweating Frank and looked quickly around at Terry.

When Terry's scream of 'copper' reached Frank's ears, he had just managed to lift the barrow handles and, in the process, had lost his balance. He watched petrified as barrow and bricks slipped over the edge of the scaffold boards. As

they plummeted to the ground, Frank never really understood how so few of the bricks actually fell out of the barrow.
The whole load seemed simply to drop. In any collection
of famous last words, Georgie's was not particularly
memorable. His question of 'Where?' was followed by a
sickening thud.

Frank practically fell down the ladders and he had caught
up with Terry by the time that lad had reached the wire
fence. Once in the street, though, his criminal instincts served
him in good stead.

'Wait,' he called to Terry. 'What's 'appened to that bloody
copper?'

'Dunno. I shouldn't fink 'e knew we were there, 'e's probably just walked on,' panted Terry in reply.

'Let's go back for Georgie. I fink 'e might be 'urt.'

With no little courage, particularly on the part of Terry,
who was all for a spot of blind terror, the couple returned
to the scene. Georgie lay in a pool of blood and could never
be mistaken for anything other than very dead.

'Let's get 'im out of 'ere,' said Frank.

'Why?' winced Terry.

'We'll put 'im in the road and say 'e's been 'it by a car.'

'Yes, but why?'

'Don't keep saying "Why"! Look, 'e might get some in-
surance or somefink like that.'

'Well, that ain't gonna do 'im much good, is it?'

'Aw, Terry! You are a real right bottleless git! Will you
just get an 'old of 'is legs and we'll carry 'im into the next
street? There's an 'ole under that fence and we can just slide
'im frue.'

This whole operation took around ten minutes and still
fortune favoured the pair. There was no sign of the security
guard, nor of anyone else for that matter. Damson Street
was part of a great slum-clearance programme. Other than
a few learner drivers going backwards and forwards, and

the occasional courting couple making much the same movement, it was usually empty. In fact, the security guard, whom Terry in his panic had mistaken for a copper, was quietly reading in his hut. It was nearly time for him to punch a clock card and then he could slip away for another pint.

The lads had agreed that Georgie should be made to appear the victim of a hit-and-run driver. They nervously parked both his car and his body in Damson Street. Frank phoned for an ambulance from the nearby phone box. As an afterthought, he also decided to call Georgie's dad.

'So if it hadn't been for that copper at the building site, Georgie would still be alive now?' observed Sidney on the telephone.

'Well, yeh, if yer put it like that, I s'pose 'e would,' replied a puzzled Frank.

'Right! We'll sue!' said the ever-optimistic Sid.

Frank shrugged as he replaced the receiver. He considered he had worry enough at the moment, without contemplating litigation.

'Why on earth didn't you tell me the truth in the first place?' asked the incredulous Inspector Watts. 'You must have realized you couldn't possibly hope to get away with that story.'

'Well, guv'nor, we've 'ad five ropes altogether from that building site.'

'So?'

'Well, we fort we might get into trouble for it.'

Watts closed his eyes and ever so slowly buried his face in his hands.

The following day I reported for duty at 2 p.m. and listened in fascination as Inspector Watts recited the story to me. I did not see Steve until later that afternoon when he returned from a day spent at Crown Court. I soon realized that he had not heard how the previous evening's drama had finally ended.

'The two boys eventually put their hands up to it, Steve,' I said. 'You were right all along – he wasn't killed in Damson Street.'

'I think they ought to go on the sheet for criminal damage as well,' he replied ruefully, as I finished telling the story.

'What on earth for?'

'Well, God knows what was on that wheelbarrow that I fell over, but it's totally ruined my trousers.'

A Royal Wedding

I left the station at 7 p.m. and drove wearily home. It had been a very long day indeed. We had begun work at seven o'clock that morning and my legs were complaining, from hips to ankles.

Joan, my wife, had, in her own opinion, 'a great idea': 'Christine and I will leave you nice and quiet and we will trot off to Hyde Park to see the Royal Firework Display. You can therefore have a nice early night.'

The reason for my family's concern was that, in common with a few thousand other London coppers', my alarm clock would be set for 3 a.m. the following morning. An hour after that, most of us would be parading at our stations for the Royal Wedding of Prince Charles and Lady Diana.

'It doesn't work out as easy as that,' I complained. 'Just because I have to get up in the middle of the night, doesn't mean I'll sleep any better if I go to bed early. I'm not a camel.'

'I know you're not, dear,' Joan said, patiently. 'Camels store food, not sleep. All I am asking you to do is to try. A warm bath, a glass of hot milk and you'll be asleep before your head hits the pillow.'

'If I am going to drug myself into oblivion, then I'll do it my own way, thank you. I've not drunk hot milk since I had scarlet fever at the age of five, and as far as I can remember the fever was marginally better than the milk.'

'All right, have a couple of whiskies if you must, but

134

remember, you'll be buying a night-long sleep with a day-long headache.'

Not having a satisfactory answer to that, I assumed my 'wise look'. This is an expression that I adopt when I wish it to appear that I have taken into account all of the options, considered them, then arrived at a carefully planned decision. It was also time for them to depart.

'Now, if you two will kindly leave me in peace, I'll prepare for sleep. Good night!'

We said our farewells and mother and daughter strode away towards the railway station. I poured myself a large scotch.

Sleep was in fact a very real problem. If I know that I have to wake particularly early then I hardly sleep at all. The more I try to sleep, the more desperate the situation becomes. I laid out uniform, shirt and shoes for a quick getaway in the morning and I slipped between the sheets around 9.30 p.m. I clearly remember looking at the clock at 10 p.m., then I must have fallen into a deep slumber.

The bell cut through my unconscious state. I reached out instinctively and switched off the alarm. I felt as though I had only just climbed into bed. I swung my feet down to the floor and sat wearily on the edge of the mattress. Stupid alarm, it was still ringing. At this rate it would wake the rest of the household. I looked quickly behind me and was surprised to see the other half of the bed still vacant. Three in the morning is a bit late for fireworks, I thought. I could not somehow join together the loose pieces of my brain: it seemed fragmented. God, I do hate early mornings! First I must stop that bell. I again reached out to the clock, and then I noticed the time – 10.35 p.m. It was not the alarm that was ringing – it was the telephone!

I staggered to the top of the stairs and almost fell down the fourteen steps. I shuffled along the passage and into the living-room. I circuited the table and dodged around an armchair. It was somewhere around this stage that I realized that the blasted phone had ceased to ring. I picked up the receiver just in case – nothing but the dialling tone. I even spoke three anxious 'Hullos' – all to no avail. I muttered my way into the kitchen and gulped down a glass of water. The bell again! Again the mad obstacle race to the telephone, but this time I captured a voice.

'Hullo, Harry?'

I recognized the cheery tones of Tug Wilson. Tug has been a civilian night-duty telephonist at Wharf Road for the last twenty-five years.

'Yer?' I answered, suspiciously.

'Tug here. The chief inspector has ordered that we confirm that everyone who is on duty at the wedding tomorrow knows for sure the times that they are to parade. I'm just checking that you know yours.'

'You are what!!!?' I exploded. 'Do you have any idea what the bloody time is? You've virtually woken me up to ask me why I was in bed so early! Is he there?'

'Who?'

'The chief inspector, of course!'

'No. He's no fool, you know,' said Tug. 'He's gone out again. Everyone wants to speak to him.'

'I bet they do! Well, just add me to the list. And if I'm late in the morning, tell them it's because some cretin phoned and kept me awake half the night!'

'Will do. G'night.'

Poor Tug. Everyone had blasted him and it really wasn't his fault. At least his phone call had concentrated my mind. I no longer worried if I would have sufficient sleep, nor did I worry if I would hear the alarm. All my conscious thoughts were aimed at a chief inspector who for the first time in his life had decided to become efficient.

*

Minutes later, it seemed, the real alarm assailed the quiet, still air of my bedroom. A quick shower and shave was all that was required before setting off for work. Breakfast was to be provided by the force. We were to be, as many coppers would claim, 'force-fed'.

A quick inspection and briefing took place. A few minutes later, we were embarking on a coach that transported us to a mammoth feeding centre just off the Old Kent Road. This centre is a huge warehouse that is big on food and short on ventilation. The attempt to demolish sausages, bacon, chips, beans, rolls, marmalade, coffee and chocolate biscuit at 4.45 a.m. in that atmosphere was just a little too much for me. I declined any food and simply settled for a coffee. I am always amazed how many people can eat with such gusto at that hour of the day. There must have been three hundred men and women all tucking in cheerfully.

I sat packed tightly at a table with twenty of my colleagues. Realizing that dawn was now breaking, I decided to take my coffee outside into the cool street. It was at this precise moment that I dropped my cup. The forces that are released by a dropped cup of coffee are truly astonishing. The explosion was awesome, then the language was breathtaking! I sought refuge from the abuse of the victims in the cheers and applause of those who had escaped the deluge. Wishing the ground would open up, I slunk outside into the street and sat on the kerb. Not a good start to the day.

Coppers of both sexes were now emerging from the centre in ever-increasing numbers. The morning was breaking fine and sunny and the street was quiet and cool. A whole row of policemen and policewomen sat on the kerbstones like gnomes in a garden. Soon the Wharf Road contingent were all present and we again boarded the coach. Some fifteen minutes later found us in the Strand, where we were to remain for the whole of the wedding procession and ceremony.

137

The crowd was already six deep on our arrival, with many people still curled up in their sleeping bags. Flags, balloons, newspapers and banners lay all over and around the assembled throng. 'Prince Charles Can Eat Three Shredded Wheats' read the most dominating sign. There was increasing activity on the route itself, council workers and cleaners busying themselves around. Slowly the crowd was awakening, although many of the standing and sitting members had been denied the luxury of sleep. We relieved the tired night-duty officers who were lining the route and I searched my sleep-starved brain for something to say to the throng. 'Get to know your crowd,' we had been told at the briefing, 'and let them get to know you.' That is all very well, but what can one say as an ice-breaker in a situation like that? 'Morning, my name's Harry and I'm supposed to watch you lot like a hawk'? Hardly, but perhaps a little leg-pulling might go down well. I tried it; it didn't work. Clearing my throat, I pulled myself up to my full five feet, nine inches.

'I don't quite know how to tell this to you, but they've eloped.'

The trouble was that a sizeable group of the crowd was still only half awake.

'What did that copper say?' they yawned.

'They've eloped.'

The yawns died.

Five yards further down the Strand was my old friend Bootsie Hill. He sidled up to me and whispered, 'The order said get to know them, not send them all home, you idiot!'

I took the point.

The first couple of hours slipped by and everyone was now wide awake. The crowd had reached the stage when they needed to cheer, and cheer they did. They applauded everything that moved, regardless of what it was, or in which direction it travelled. In fact one of the greatest receptions

of the day was reserved for the rubbish cart. The solitary
black man sitting on the back received more cheers than
any foreign head of state. He loved every second of it. He
acknowledged each burst of cheering with a huge smile and
a gracious wave, as if to the manner born.

Soon the first of the guests' cars began to roll by. An
occasional car slowly developed into a steady stream of
traffic. In the main they were chauffeur-driven limousines.
One of the few exceptions was an old Morris 1000cc Traveller
Estate. It was falling apart with rust and probably had a
second-hand value just a little below the two top hats perched
inside it. The four occupants were dressed to the nines. They
resembled Cinderella after the coach had turned back into
a pumpkin.

The soldiers were now taking up positions along the route.
This caused some hold-ups to the smooth flow of guests'
cars. During one such hold-up the comedian Spike Milligan
alighted from his car and went on a walk-about among the
crowd. Suddenly the cars resumed the journeys and Spike
had great difficulty in gaining access to his vehicle. Gales
of laughter swept down the Strand as the chauffeur leapt
out to assist him. A young American girl standing close by
asked me who he was. I explained that Spike was a much-
loved British lunatic.

'Well, why doesn't each car have a number on it?' she
asked. 'Then all we would have to do is to look down at
a programme to see who they are.'

'I think, judging by the heavily darkened glass in some
of the cars, that would not suit many of the guests,' I
explained.

Some various members of the Royal Family began to pass.
Dukes, duchesses, princes and princesses, some familiar,
many unknown. The clattering-hooved sound of the Household Cavalry indicated that the Queen herself was close by.
The formal applause and cheers that greeted the groom

seemed in a direct contrast to the oohs and ahhs that accompanied the bride. Stage one had arrived at a successful conclusion. I suddenly remembered the old nursery rhyme about the Grand Old Duke of York:

> He had ten thousand men.
> He marched them to the top of the hill
> Then he marched them down again.

Well, I may not have seen quite ten thousand go up to St Paul's, but nevertheless it had been a pretty fair number. Soon they would all be coming down again.

Those of us lining the route now had ninety minutes in which to stretch our legs and relax. We had discovered from several members of the crowd that a deputy police commissioner had stated on television that policemen would be giving away sweets to the spectators en route. 'Where's yer sweets?' we were constantly being asked. Even disc jockeys on the radio had become caught up in the act: 'Don't forget to ask the policeman for a sweet,' they chirruped between records.

Most of the coppers looked at each other in genuine puzzlement.

'Have you got any sweets, Boots?' I asked.

'No – have you?' he replied.

I lightly patted my pockets in a gesture of emptiness.

'No –' I began. But wait, there was something there. Then I remembered. Two months earlier, on the Trooping of the Colour, I had suffered a sore throat. I had bought four ounces of cough candies and I had just six of them left. These sole survivors were now fermented together in one sweating lump. I removed them from my pocket and gingerly broke off two. Bootsie received his, not without suspicion, and I bravely popped the other into my mouth. Except for a slight coating of dust, it seemed quite edible.

'Oy! How about ours, then?' called a young man from the middle of the pavement.

I tossed the remaining clump across to him and he accepted them gratefully.

My legs were now making their first complaint of the day. In order to alleviate this I walked a small patrol of about fifty yards in both directions. The crowd appeared the same mixture wherever I looked. I had covered most of the grand occasions in the last thirty years but this crowd was undoubtedly the happiest that I had ever seen. It seemed that everyone was determined to make it a good day.

Some thirty minutes later, my attention was drawn by the young man to whom I had given the sweets. He waved and raised his hand rapidly a couple of times.

'I've got no more sweets, mate, sorry,' I answered.

'Sweets!' snorted Bootsie. 'He's not talking about sweets. Look at his wrist, man, it's stiff. He's talking about a drink!'

At first I refused to believe our luck. I could certainly have murdered a pint but I did not want my hopes to be falsely raised.

'What actually is he saying, Boots?' I whispered.

'Dunno,' said Bootsie, as he tried desperately to decipher the signals.

Finally we both understood. Our delightful young friend had obtained two foaming pints of bitter and he was asking us where we would like to drink them!

'Well, with the greatest goodwill in the world, Boots, we can't drink them here in front of the crowd. We'd have more television coverage than the bride. How about the alley at the back there?'

I pointed to a narrow street at the rear of the crowd and Bootsie was already squeezing through the crush barriers before I had dropped my arm! I followed quickly behind.

A few yards down the alley was a flight of stone steps. These led up to a padlocked doorway. Bootsie picked up a newspaper and spread it across the highest step. We both sat down and secreted ourselves back into the doorway. Our benefactor then handed us both pints. He had hardly spilt a drop.

'Oh you lovely boy!' exclaimed Bootsie. 'How much do we owe you?'

'Forget it,' came the reply. He turned and looked at me. 'You gave me some sweets, remember?'

Bootsie looked gratefully at the young man, then happily towards me. I raised my glass to the youth.

'Best move you've made today, dad,' said Bootsie (he always calls me 'dad' at times of great emotion).

'As ye sow, so ye shall reap, son,' I said wisely. 'Cheers.'

I have rarely tasted a pint that I enjoyed more. I did falter for just a second, though. It was at the moment that Bootsie said: 'You know, we're just like a couple of old vagrants. We're sitting on a newspaper, in a doorway, drinking our booze, which we haven't paid for, and trying to avoid capture.'

Draining our glasses, we handed them back to the young man and thanked him profusely. We squeezed our way through the crowd and took up our places in the Strand gutter. Even my legs now felt better.

It was shortly afterwards that I began to feel quite hungry. The absence of any breakfast was beginning to take its toll of me. Since our arrival in the street that morning, people had plied us with all manner of goodies. So far I had refused, but I was now ready to accept the next offer that was made to me. It was now nearly sixteen hours since I had eaten and my stomach had the feeling that my throat had been cut.

'Wanna bitta pie, mate?'

Almost on cue came the offer from a red-haired, off-duty bus conductress. She stood near the rear of the pavement.

'Thanks, luv, yes, I will, please.'

142

I gratefully reached over the crush barriers towards the tinfoil-wrapped package. We stretched out towards each other like doomed lovers in a ballet, but we were still about eighteen inches short of actual contact. She tried again and this time her hand passed over yet another couple of heads, and mine responded. We had almost touched, when a loud 'pop' indicated to me that my belt had burst. My trousers instantly slackened and dropped from my waist to my hips. Less than fifteen yards away, two huge, mobile gantries ominously held the television cameras of both the BBC and ITV. There was more than an outside chance that my 'Y' fronts would soon be flashed around the world. I withdrew my hand quickly and grabbed at my trouser tops. The pie fell pitifully between two elderly sisters who looked very much like book-ends.

'That's the quickest I've ever seen you move,' said Bootsie.

'My belt's just broken; the buckle has sheared completely off!'

'Well, all you need is some string,' he answered, soothingly.

'String! Where the hell am I going to find string from around here?'

'Well, you'll just have to use your initiative, won't you? If you don't, your bum will become the best-known London landmark after Big Ben.' He gestured towards the TV cameras. 'Go along and ask them blokes. They have just about everything in their equipment.'

I will say one thing for Bootsie, he does just occasionally have a good idea. With my hands held firmly in my pockets, I quickly covered the few yards to the cameras. A swift explanation and I was soon in the huge van where most of their equipment is carried. Those vast carriers and their crews are incredible. They obtain pictures from the street outside and bounce them from space-suspended satellites. At that very moment the sights and sounds from the Strand were penetrating 1000 million television sets around the world.

143

They have the most sophisticated equipment imaginable and the high level of skill needed to use it. They have efficiency, proficiency, prowess and technology. They have expertise, they have science, they have technique. What they don't have is a piece of string.

'We definitely should have a piece here somewhere, officer,' said one of the crew.

Drawers were opened, clothing was searched, lockers were turned out, but no string could be found.

'Well, don't worry about it,' I muttered, unconvincingly. 'I'm sure I'll find a piece somewhere.'

I turned to leave but the older member of the staff would not hear of it.

'I've an idea. Take off your belt.'

I complied. He examined it carefully, then approached a padlocked cupboard. The sign on the door read: 'Danger – Radioactivity'. He opened the door and removed from it a roll of adhesive tape. He bound it quickly and efficiently around the belt and buckle. In no time at all he returned it to me.

'Good as new,' he smiled.

Well, it looked okay and it certainly worked all right, but a radioactive belt?

'It won't sort of . . . ? Well, you know,' I stammered.

'Of course it won't. It's only an ordinary piece of adhesive tape. Just take it off as soon as you can, that's all.'

'Thanks, thanks very much,' I murmured.

I walked out of that van holding my stomach in so much that it made my back ache. Easing my way through the crowd, I returned to the kerbside. The distant cheers indicated that the wedding procession was returning from St Paul's. Soon the Strand was packed with pageantry. It had taken around ninety minutes for the guests to pass on their way to the Cathedral. Their return was easily four times faster.

'It's because the pubs are open,' explained Bootsie to a gullible old lady in the front of the crowd.

All police on the route had been asked to face the crowd as the procession passed by them. On the whole they did. That is, if one does not include the swift glance over each shoulder at the bride and groom.

Soon the last carriage had rolled by, the final car had purred home and the road sweepers had descended like sparrows on the horse dung.

'We're all going for a snack, lads,' called out an inspector. 'This way.'

I kept a close eye on the sweepers!

He led us instead to a large building in the Strand that had been temporarily leased as a feeding centre for the police. Here a pork pie, a couple of large sausages and an apple did their best to soothe my rumbling stomach. If the food was welcome, the chance to sit down was bliss. I removed my shoes and savoured my sausages in comfort. Forty-five minutes later we were told that we would be on duty on Westminster Bridge for the 'going-away' part of the ceremony. The royal couple were due to leave Buckingham Palace sometime after four o'clock and drive to Waterloo Station. I replaced my shoes, tunic and tie with something less than enthusiasm. From the Strand to Westminster Bridge is only about half a mile, but there had already been a noticeable change in the weather. The high, hazy cloud of the morning had now cleared and the sun beat fiercely down. Taking up a position on the east side of the bridge, again in the gutter, we faced the crowd. Because of the formality of the occasion, we wore our tunics instead of summer-issue shirts. We were becoming more uncomfortable at each passing minute. The morning had been very enjoyable, but I felt that the afternoon was about to become a drag. I was prophetically right.

The 'get to know your crowd' directive had been comparatively easy in the Strand. On Westminster Bridge the task could not have been performed by a computer. Bootsie and I had no fewer than six changes of position. We began on the north end of the bridge in the shade of Boadicea's statue and we finished at the south end near the steps of County Hall. Each time we moved I felt that I should take my part of the crowd with me. 'Now come on, you lot, you're my crowd, y'know. Fall in and I'll march you to a new position over the bridge!' I had reached the stage where rivulets of sweat were streaming into my eyes. The Thames did nothing to help, it just looked so inviting. If only I could have paddled my feet! Everything seemed geared to tantalize us. Pleasure boats were forming an endless procession on the water, their bow waves dancing a thousand reflections in the over-bright sun. Girls wore gossamer-like dresses and kids licked ice-creams. Our chat and bonhomie of the morning had practically vanished. We said very little, except that every few minutes I would exclaim, 'Bloody hell but it's hot, Boots.'

Bootsie never replied. He knew it was hot, he did not need me to tell him. Just occasionally, in order not to bore him, I would vary the dialogue: 'I'm absolutely knackered, Boots.'

This would sometimes draw a 'You look it' out of him, but by and large he was indifferent.

Another drawback to our position on the bridge was the proximity of Big Ben. It chimed out each quarter hour in solemn tone. By four o'clock we had been on duty for twelve hours and we were wilting fast. The procession from the palace was obviously late. Our indicator for this news was the Good Year airship. It had constantly circled over the royal route with its cameras loaded like a helicopter gunship. Around 4.30 p.m. it changed direction from Vauxhall and moved deliberately towards the palace. The honeymoon was finally under way.

146

'Git yer speshully approved soo-veneer badges. De only badges wot's bin approved by Prince Charles an' carryin' 'is per-sun-nal sig-nit-cha. Only ten pence! Ten pence only!' I looked for the voice and saw a brown-toothed, stubbly-cheeked cockney, slight of build and black-capped. 'Every one of 'em contains the per-sun-nal sig-nit-cha of der fu-cha King of England. Only ten pence! Value of der year!'

'Why are they only ten pence, then?' asked an inquisitive blue-rinsed matron.

''Is 'ighniss's speshull request, a' course. Lettum go fer only ten pence, 'e sed. I want everyone ter 'ave wun, 'e sed.'

I watched in utter amazement as he made a dozen sales in less than two minutes. I think when I leave the force I will sell goods to crowds from suitcases. There truly is one born every minute!

The cheers and the Household Cavalry indicated to me that our day was nearly over. Soon on the bridge came the royal couple – soon we could go home! As the open carriage neared the south end of the bridge, Prince Charles appeared to see the welcome signs in the ward windows of nearby St Thomas's Hospital. He pointed quickly up to the building and spoke briefly to his bride. She turned around and both of them waved a warm greeting of acknowledgement. A nice touch, I thought.

The pageant cantered smoothly out of sight. The crowd, many of whom had had a longer day than even the police, began swiftly to melt away. I glanced up at Big Ben: 5 p.m. With any luck we should be away very soon. Coppers now stood around in talkative groups, having found new energy from their impending departure. Dismissal orders were given and one by one coaches arrived to whisk away scores of police. By 5.45 p.m. the only group left on the bridge was the Wharf Road contingent. Why?

'Sorry,' said control, 'but we cannot find your coach. Don't worry, though, we will!'

'Sod this, Boots,' I cursed. 'I'm going to get a bus back.'

That, in fact, was easier said than done. Bus services had been temporarily withdrawn throughout the ceremonial area and they were only now beginning to flow again. Needless to say, they were also full of the dispersing crowd. The twenty officers from Wharf Road were now at the 'severely muttering' stage. There is not a greater muttering animal in the whole of creation than a copper who considers he has been neglected by his seniors. I personally was beyond a mutter. Bootsie and I just leaned against the balustrades of the bridge and sulked.

It was while we were in the depths of depression that a smart, slim fellow in his thirties strode by. He passed a few yards beyond us and then returned and stared at me.

'Isn't tha name PC Cole?' he queried in a strong Yorkshire accent.

'Well, er, yes, it is,' I replied, waking up a little.

'Ah thought so. Ah've read tha book and Ah recognize thee picture.'

'Well, you're the first one who ever has. Even my mother didn't know me.'

'Ah niver forget a face. Good-dee!' And off he walked.

'Hey, Boots!' I nudged him firmly. 'How about that? A fan! It's the first one I've ever had! I'm going to tell everyone about it when we get on the coach!'

'D'you know what I've been thinking about?' asked Bootsie, by way of reply.

As he was obviously not remotely interested in my solitary fan, I could do little else but reply, 'No, what?'

'A pint! A real long cool pint! The first and second probably won't even touch the sides of my throat, but I'll really enjoy the third!' He looked at his watch. 'They've been open now for twenty minutes. How about a quick couple before we go home?'

'Well, that would just about save my afternoon. But I'm

not stopping too long, mind you.' (I had been in pubs with Boots before.) 'Just a couple, then away. Okay?'

'Okay!'

At 6.15 p.m. I could stand it no longer. A number 184 bus stopped at the fare stage at the foot of the bridge.

'I'm getting this bus back. We'll be here all bloody night otherwise.'

No one else seemed to show the same initiative, so I slipped quickly into a seat on my own, leaving behind the rest of my colleagues. The driver pressed his button and both doors hissed closed. We could not move off for a few minutes owing to the volume of traffic. A loud rapping caused me to look up. A smirking Bootsie pointed to a coach that had stopped immediately behind the bus. Already most of our group had boarded. I ran to the front of the bus and begged the driver to allow me to alight. He consented with an air of extreme graciousness and once again the doors hissed.

When I finally climbed aboard our coach, I was, of course, the last to arrive. Bootsie was in the midst of recounting to the ensemble my conversation with my 'fan'. His accent was abysmal but, even worse, he lied blatantly.

'Then this bloke comes up to him and says, "Ah tha PC Cole?" "I am," said Harry, over the moon because someone has finally recognized him. "Well, tha lukes a lot *older* than tha picture."'

'Boots, you bloody liar! He never said any such thing!'

My protests were in vain. It was pretty obvious which version the coach preferred.

Fifteen minutes later we were back at Wharf Road. Our uniforms were quickly placed in our lockers and soon we were hot-footing it round to the Duke of Sutherland. We pushed at the saloon-bar door, mildly surprised that on such a hot night it should be closed. It did not budge. We looked at each other anxiously and pushed once again, only this time much harder. Still no response.

'Not only is the door closed but the whole bloody pub is closed!' cried Bootsie. 'What's the time?'

I glanced panic-stricken at my watch. 'It's a quarter to seven! It should have opened an hour and fifteen minutes ago! What could have gone wrong, Boots?'

'They've got an extension to midnight because of the wedding!' he exclaimed. 'They don't open until half past seven!'

'Boots, I've stood on my feet for almost fourteen hours today. I simply cannot stand for another forty-five minutes to wait for a pub to open, not even the Sutherland. I'm going home!'

We sadly parted company and forty minutes later I lay in a warm bath, drinking a tin of even warmer beer. I wondered why drinking beer at home is never as enjoyable as drinking it in a pub.

It's not even so good as sitting on a newspaper in a doorway, especially when someone else has paid.

A Few Delinquents

In law, a juvenile is anyone under the age of seventeen years. The age of criminal responsibility is at present ten years. It should therefore follow that any youngster who breaks the law between those two ages is a juvenile offender. This is not quite the case.

It would be as well at this stage for anyone wishing to understand the complexities of adolescent crime, to realize that there is an additional stratum to the law that relates to juveniles. It is an extremely important stratum and one which any police recruit, for example, would be well advised to study before embarking on a law-enforcing career. This additional law, while having no official place in the statute book, is nevertheless practised and accepted by 98 per cent of the parents in this country. This law is referred to as the OCOPK theory. Translated, it becomes the Our-Children-Other-Peoples-Kids law. It is absolutely impossible to deal with any young offender and not to be confronted with this law.

Subscribers to OCOPK have decidedly strong views. They consider that the vast majority of kids in this country deserve a hard, swift kick up the bum. They recognize that the nation is going rapidly to the dogs and they offer some interesting theories on how this has arisen and how best to correct the slide. The first symptom of this decline, OCOPK points out, is the total breakdown of classroom discipline. 'Teachers have no control nowadays over their classes. The kids are allowed to do just as they please. In my day, you got the cane for just looking up from your work book.'

OCOPK members further point out that in-bred respect for the law by the young has also diminished. They will then offer the following reason for their own strict adherence: 'When I was a child, whenever a policeman caught you doing anything wrong, he would always give you a clip around the earhole. When you arrived home and complained to your dad, he'd always give you another one.'

W-e-l-l, yes. But I do begin to have a few reservations at this stage. That statement seems to imply that this duplicated beating was inflicted with some regularity. Okay, it could possibly happen *once* to a child, I will agree. A copper may well have given him a belt around the ear and he would have duly arrived home with his head ringing. There a doting father would presumably have given him another, this time on the opposite side of the head, in an attempt to redress the balance. But what manner of fool ventures home on more than one occasion with a throbbing earhole, knowing that immediately he recites a tale of brutality and injustice, he will receive yet another beating? I somehow feel that a pinch of salt is in order here.

Perhaps my own moral character is weak, but once would have been enough for me. I would have been prepared to concoct all manner of lying excuses for the throbbing ear. Perhaps I was kicked while stopping a runaway horse? Even injured while rescuing a one-legged man from a collapsing building. It may well have been caused by the gigantic wheels of a red London bus, just before I snatched up a blind baby only inches from its path. Whatever gallant reason I might have given, it most certainly would never have been put down to a belligerently overbearing member of the local constabulary. Not if it was going to cost me a wallop around the ear, it wouldn't!

Anyway, let us leave aside this mythical masochistic

cretin. OCOPK seeks to redress this imbalance in youthful crime by attacking the offenders with every penal deterrent possible. It wishes to do this by strengthening controls and giving a free rein to every teacher, copper, shopowner, youth-club leader, vicar and harassed old lady. It wishes to come down on every pain-in-the-arse-kid like a ton of bricks.

OCOPK does not seek for its own members' children to be chastised. It is a well-known fact among OCOPK members that their own children are above reproach. No, what OCOPK requires is that society in general, and the law in particular, should really get stuck into everyone else's kids. As every caring parent knows, it is always everyone else's kids who cause all this trouble.

This was never more apparent to me than when I arrested my first juveniles. Two fifteen-year-old lads who had broken into a block of offices, not for any specific reason. It was more a venture of opportunity. If there were anything worth nicking then they would consider taking it, if not, well, nothing was lost, only time, and they had plenty of that. They were really quite philosophical about it.

'Do the parents know that they have been arrested?' asked the station officer as soon as we entered the station.

'No, sergeant, they were only nicked a few minutes ago.'

'Very well. Go straight around to both addresses and dig out the parents.'

What I did not realize that evening was that my experience would be typical of every young copper's who had ever found himself in that situation. Even the dialogue hardly varies.

Some fifteen minutes later I called on the Kemp family and the first of the parents then got into the back of the police car. She was the mother of the older boy. In many families, bailing out the kids is classified as woman's work. It is a little like cleaning the gas-stove or cooking the dinner.

'Little Darren has been nicked again, Lil. You'd better nip down to the station and bail him out.'

Lil will sit in the back of the police car in almost total silence. Then, after a while, she will ask one question. Surprisingly, it will not be, 'What did he do?' or even 'Where was it?' No, her first question will almost invariably be, 'Who was he with?'

When you reply, 'Dean Willmot', she will nod her head vigorously. 'I knew it!' she will say. 'I knew it! How many times have I told him about that sodding Dean. I bet every time that he goes out with that bloody kid so he winds up in trouble. My Darren would never do anyone any harm. Everybody will tell you that, but he gets with that sodding Dean and he somehow gets led. I just can't understand why he does it, he's got a lovely home an' everything. It's her, you know, it's his mother. It's her that I blame. Well, what can you expect? She just lets him run wild. You can't blame the boy if his mother is like that. My Darren won't play with him any more though, oh no! I'll assure you of that. That sodding Dean wants putting away, I reckon. You just wait until my husband sees him! He'll kill him, he will, he'll bloody kill him!'

Now the very first time that this is said to a young constable, he will believe every word. Why shouldn't he? He will have visions of 'Dean's mum' being a cross between Lucrezia Borgia and Ma Baker. Every night the wicked woman obviously sends out her young son on an extravaganza of crime and the dastardly Dean – Svengali-like – must regularly hypnotize poor Darren into accompanying him.

'There is no doubt about it,' the constable will think, 'society needs protecting from such as the Willmots.' He will then feel a warmness towards poor Lil now sitting lost in thought in the back of the police car. If there were any justice in the world at all, she would never find herself in

154

this situation. How worrying it must be to have a son who is so saint-like by nature, yet whose very disposition is being eroded away by such an evil family as the Willmots.

I stopped the vehicle outside a tenement block and left Lil still meditating on the back seat. I then reassured her in my best telephone voice and climbed the seventy-odd stairs to the Willmots' flat. (That was something that I learnt that night: people who live on the ground floors of blocks of flats never receive visits from the police. I have now spent thirty years knocking on doors and I swear that they have always been at the top!)

I manifested my burning indignation at the way that Lil had been treated by rapping angrily on the Willmots' front door. No one answered. I rapped again, this time even louder and longer. Somewhere in the depths of the flat I heard a WC flush. A few seconds later the door was opened by a thin, balding, middle-aged man. He held a *Sporting Life* in his unwashed hands and his braces dangled. His eyes narrowed as they looked at me.

'Yeh?'

'Mr Willmot?'

'Yeh?'

'Mr Willmot, we have your son down at Wharf Road police station. He was arrested – by myself, in point of fact – for office-breaking. We now require the presence of one, or both, of his parents. He will eventually be released into your custody while the case is being investigated.'

I had a rather smug feeling that Mr Willmot was quite impressed with the delivery of that little speech. I waited eagerly for his response. Mr Willmot then turned his head and bellowed irritably back into the flat.

'ROSE!'

'YEH?' came back an equally irritable reply.

'Go dahn to the nick with this geezer. Dean's in trouble ag'in, office-breakin' or somefink. Though Gawd knows

155

why he wants to break into a bleedin' office, 'e can't bleedin'
well read!' Turning his attention back to me, he looked
me up and down. He sniffed loudly. ''Ang abaht, John,
she won't be long. She's just putting on her stays.'

He then slammed the door with a force that vibrated
the whole block. At first I was going to return to the car
and wait there for Rosie Willmot. But when I thought more
about it, I realized I would never be sure if she was actually
joining us at all. She might simply take her 'stays' off again
and remain indoors.

Five minutes later the door opened and Rosie Willmot
appeared. My first impression of her was one of sheer
weight. It was not that she was fat, she wasn't. It was simply
that she looked so bloody heavy. Absolutely everything
about her looked heavy, even her hair! She wore a maroon-
coloured dress that made just a token curve in at the waist.
Her bust gave the impression of fossilized pillow-cases, while
her champagne-bottle legs seemed to have been driven
fiercely down into her shoes. The thin, stiletto-type heels
of these shoes were obviously a remarkable piece of engi-
neering: everything of this truly massive woman seemed to
balance delicately on those two tiny, half-square-inch
supports.

Rosie Willmot did not waste time, she came straight to
the point. 'Well, who was he with this time?'

'Who was "who" with?'

'Why, Dean, o' course. Who the bleedin' hell d'you think
I mean?'

'Oh, I see. Well, he was with Darren Kemp.'

'Oh I might 'a' known it! Who else *would* he be with!
That fucking Darren – excuse my language – he'll get my
young Dean hung, he will, you'll see if he don't. Still, you
can't blame the kid, that's what I say. You've only got
to look at his mother to see where the trouble really lays.
Out every night, she don't give a sod for that boy. I wouldn't

mind –' and at this point her voice rose an octave in emphasis – 'but how many times have his dad and me told him not to have anything to do with that bloody Kemp kid? He's bad news, he is. My Dean, if he's left to himself, is a really smashing boy, everyone says so. But whenever he gets with that fucking Kemp kid – excuse my language – so he's in trouble. His father'll kill him when he gets home, he'll kill him, he will.'

I was now completely confused. How could each of these kids fulfil the role that the parents apparently believed they did? I was very apprehensive about our return drive to Wharf Road. I thought that they would be bound to be at each other's throats. I need not have worried. Each woman sat in the back of the car just as if the other did not exist. Lil Kemp looked unblinking out of the offside window while Rosie Willmot looked out of the nearside. I did give a little thought to some conversation, but my nerve cracked and I changed the first two syllables into a cough. Neither woman appeared even to have heard it.

It was soon obvious that both ladies knew not only as much about juvenile procedure as the station officer but they also knew infinitely more than I did. I kept discreetly quiet during the whole operation. Some twenty minutes later they and their respective sons all silently left the building together. It was like a mutes' convention.

'Bloody hell, sarge!' I exclaimed, as the door closed behind them. I began eagerly to recite to him the details of the conversations that I had shared with both mums. I was quite full of it and I waited expectantly for his response of astonishment. He was totally unimpressed.

'You will find out that they are all like that, son,' he murmured, slowly shaking his head. 'It's never their children, it's always other people's kids.'

I was extremely fortunate that my first introduction to the

157

usual complexities of juvenile crime had been so comparatively uncomplicated. It is the sort of crime that in any inner-city area will occupy the majority of a street copper's time. It has been that way for many years now and there is no sign of any change.

No section of society is subject to so many contradictions and anomalies, as is the wayward child. No section of society suffers from such a Himalayan volume of useless help. No section of society draws so many well-meaning, ill-informed, crack-brained, eccentric dunderheads, all with their own pet theories of how best to cope with the wayward adolescent. Just as the children of the 1960s believed that they were the first generation to discover sex, so there is a whole mass of academics who believe that they alone hold the panacea for the juvenile offender.

These juvenile offenders, as a general rule, divide into two well-separated groups. When children of the first group are arrested, the trauma of the arrest plus the formalities at the police station provide them with the necessary shock. Most of these will straighten themselves out, rarely getting into trouble again.

The second group has no such inhibitions about police stations. Yet even so, a sizeable proportion of these youngsters will abstain from crime once they discover the opposite sex. They will swop a hand-in-the-till for a hand-in-the-blouse, so to speak. This latter group often undergoes a greater change than any other section of society. They frequently become extremely conservative in their attitudes and are often almost aggressively law-abiding. By the time they are twenty-one years of age, they would often be quite happy to see the death penalty restored for sheep-stealing.

What we are then left with is the established, long-term law-breaker, whose pedigree can often date back to his primary school days. Now while there has been no shortage of ideas and suggestions on how to cope with these youngsters, there has been a complete absence of satisfactory results.

One comparatively recent idea was the short-sharp-shock treatment. This entails youngsters' being exposed to a spell of hardship and discipline. Critics of this treatment claim that it has not worked. In fact they claim that statistics prove it has had the reverse effect. The trouble is, of course, that statistics can often be wrong when applied to the young offender.

The usual system nowadays seems to be to start with a gentle approach.

'Now, Timothy, don't you see how silly you have been to take this money?'

Timothy will rather shamefacedly nod his head in agreement. Of course he will! He will agree simply because he has been caught. Timothy will sensibly agree with just about anything that anyone says if he thinks that by so doing he might get away with it. What Timothy is no doubt thinking, if he has been stealing this money with any regularity and he has only been caught *once*, is that in reality he is not silly at all! And who is to say that he is wrong? It is precisely at this stage when most policemen feel that Timothy would be more receptive to a 'short-sharp-shock'. But by the time he is a third-year student in the academy of violent crime, it is too bloody late!

While we do not wish for Timothy to have his hands cut off, we would prefer him to know that his victims are not now among the world's happiest people. Most youngsters, of course, differ greatly. The method that works for one does not necessarily work for them all. It is, however, a sad fact that the 'good-swift-kick-up-the-bum' that was requested by OCOPK could well have worked for a great number of Timothys, *if* it had been applied early enough.

It is by no means uncommon for a youngster to have a dozen convictions behind him and still never have been deprived of a minute of his liberty. One of the worst of this type was a rather nice-looking lad named 'Frenchie'. Now just about everything to do with Frenchie was wrong. Take his name for starters, the nearest that Frenchie had ever been to France was when the juvenile court almost sent him to a remand home in Kent. Besides, he was of Cypriot descent. But he loved the name Frenchie, believing that it gave him the air of a gangsterland mystic. I have known him for all his life which, in my experience, has been one of continual and unmitigated lawlessness. Frenchie will steal just about anything from anyone. He suffers neither compunction nor compassion for any of his innumerable victims, and his one overriding personal philosophy is, 'They've got it, I ain't.' What 'they' actually have which Frenchie does not have includes such worldly treasures as pension books, bus passes, gas-meter money, thirty-shilling handbags and cheap plastic wallets.

In a fit of total frustration late one evening, I seized hold of him roughly and spun him around. We came face to face, our noses practically touching.

'You obnoxious little git!' I snarled. 'Have you ever in your whole life actually done anything for anyone? Have you ever helped anybody? Have you ever been kind to anyone?'

They were not really questions to which I expected an answer. Asking them was, I suppose, just a gesture of total failure on my part. By the frown that suddenly appeared on his face he seemed genuinely puzzled by these queries and he thought for some moments. His face then visibly brightened.

'Yeh! Yeh I have!' he exclaimed. He was now absolutely bursting with joy.

'What was it?' I demanded.

'I got an errand for an aunt once!' he replied proudly. 'That counts, don't it?'

'You got a *what*?'

'An errand! You know, taters an' greens and fings like that. My aunt wasn't well an' my mum said that she reckons I oughta go an' git some errands for 'er, so I did.'

'And that's it? That's the sum total of your entire contribution to the general happiness of this world, some "taters an' greens" for a sick aunt?'

'Yer. I dunno why you're 'aving a go at me, though. You asked me if I'd ever done anyfing for anyone, an' when I tell yer that I 'ave, you git the right needle with me! I fink that's well out of order.'

I suddenly realized that for the first time in my experience of him, Frenchie Stavoros was genuinely hurt. I am ashamed to say that I quite enjoyed it.

I did not fully realize just how hurt he was until the following day. As I entered the station in the early afternoon to begin a late-turn duty, the station officer told me that Frenchie had been waiting to see me for about half an hour.

'Frenchie Stavoros? What the hell does he want?'

'He wouldn't say,' answered the station officer indifferently. 'He just said that he wanted to speak to you.'

I strolled across the hall to the sparsely furnished waiting-room. Frenchie sat busily in the corner with a felt-tipped pen, painting his name on the freshly decorated wall.

'You an artist, Frenchie?'

'Eh!' He spun around. 'Oh, I've spoke to me mum, an' she reckons that when I once visited me gran in Cyprus I got some errands for 'er as well.'

'Right ho, son, I'll enter it on your file.'

'Okay, fanks!' he said cheerily, as he put away his pen and walked out into the afternoon sunshine.

Fortunately, not all juvenile offenders are as impenetrable as Frenchie Stavoros. Stanley Henry Ian Tompkins had every reason to hate his parents. With initials like that, he must have thought that they had determined that every one of his school days should be absolute purgatory. Therefore when his own son was born, Stanley decided to keep it simple: 'Stan' Tompkins was the only name that was entered on the birth certificate – although he soon acquired the nickname of 'Small Stan'. Somehow Stan grew up to suit my idea of that name. He was quick-witted, slight of build and brimful of confidence. He was also a crook. I am never sure what particular ingredient it is that makes some crooks likeable, but whatever it is, Stan had it by the ton. His juvenile exploits were many, yet none involved violence. All required a great deal of planning and adaptability. Stan would have earned a good living in whatever occupation he chose to follow. I always felt sad that he chose one of crime.

The first time that our paths crossed was in a fur warehouse just a few streets from the Wharf Road manor. The night watchman had awakened from a drunken slumber with an overriding desire to ease the pressure on his bladder. As he slowly eased himself from his torn armchair and back into sobriety, he was aware of a movement on the other side of the glass partition that separated his office from the stored furs. As a general rule, any break-in to a fur warehouse would only be made by a 'team' which, in turn, would need one – possibly two – vehicles. The watchman, having no great desire to risk a confrontation with any heavy mob, stealthily reached out for the office telephone and dialled the 999 emergency number. A few minutes later, the local area car, Mike 1, raced to the scene, with support from Bootsie Hill and me in Mike 3. An added bonus was the close proximity of a police dog van, which contained two Alsatians together with their handlers.

The watchman, meanwhile, had slowly eased himself through the back door of his office and was waiting for us at the main gate on our arrival.

'There's a big team of 'em,' he panted.

'How many?' asked Bootsie.

'Dunno for sure, but I'm positive that I saw at least five.'

We spread out and began to search the premises. Within less than a minute, a shout from the first floor indicated that the driver of Mike 1 had turned up something. There were further yells, then the sound of running feet.

'He's gone out through the window!'

The younger of the two dog-handlers doubled back quickly to the main gate of the building. The dog was now extremely excited, straining at the leash and barking furiously.

'Stop! Or I'll let the dog go!' I heard the handler shout.

I arrived at the gate in time to see the intruder actually increase his speed. The handler slipped the leash and the dog was away like a greyhound out of a slip. Leaping up to the fleeing figure, it seized hold of his right arm, stopping the runner dead in his tracks.

'It's Small Stan Tompkins!' exclaimed Bootsie, now seeing the suspect's face for the first time. 'Don't panic, son. He'll not hurt you if you keep still.'

Small Stan soon showed that panic was just about the last thing on his mind. He stood motionless for a moment, then, summoning up the slight total of his natural aggression, he shouted loudly at the dog, 'Down! – Sit!'

To everyone's utter astonishment, that is exactly what the animal did! It released its arm-shattering grip on Stan and, with the exception of his eagerly wagging tail, sat perfectly still, gazing open-mouthed and fondly into the young crook's face. Astonished and impressed though his audience may have been, Stan did not hang around long enough for any applause. He was away on his toes so quickly that he had disappeared into some nearby flats almost before we had gathered our wits.

'Do you know that boy then, Boots?' asked the driver of Mike 1.

'Yes,' replied Bootsie, 'I know him well. He's a strange kid, really. If we just drive around now and park outside his house, he'll get into the car with absolutely no trouble at all. Yet he somehow feels that to get captured at the scene of a break-in is a blow to his professional pride. Let him go, we can pick him up at any time. Let's look for the other four.'

'Boots, have you ever known that kid to work with anyone else?' I queried.

'That's a point, no, I haven't. He's a complete loner, he always works by himself. Let's see that nightwatchman again!'

After a few questions, the old fellow admitted that perhaps the definite sighting of five men could well have been just one small boy. Six policemen, three vehicles and two dogs then tactfully withdrew.

For the next few weeks, Stan Tompkins was to haunt me. I could barely go to an incident without Small Stan not being somehow involved in it. It is strange how this form of continuity so often happens to policemen. It is possible, for example, to go for months, even years, without a fire or an accidental death, then within the space of a few weeks there will probably be half a dozen. Likewise with people. One copper's path will continually cross that of the same villain, yet the remainder of the station personnel will probably never even have heard of the bloke. I had now reached a stage where, if I was called to a break-in and Stan was not responsible for it, I felt quite disappointed.

The peak of my involvement with Stan came some weeks later. It was as if every encounter there had been between the two of us had simply been a rehearsal for the one great finale.

There was a large factory site quite close to Camberwell

Green which a chain-store used as a temporary warehouse in the busy months before Christmas. The building had been extensively damaged by bombing during the last war and its remaining three storeys were nothing more than a makeshift adaptation of its former five floors. The roof was a rather delicate asbestos creation, and from time to time would-be intruders had been known to crash through it on to the packing cases below.

With that sort of history, the premises did not really need the silent alarm that was fitted to every few yards of the building. Word of mouth was enough to make any illegal entry to the place a fairly daunting process. When the 1.30 a.m. suspect call was therefore not immediately followed by the customary sequel – that is, 'Man through the roof' – the patrolling police car crews were noticeably impressed, and perhaps just a little disappointed.

I had been on foot duty that night and the station van which sped down the Walworth Road stopped briefly to enable me to leap aboard. It is always a welcome break for a walking copper to attend a good suspect 'shout', particularly if he is having difficulty in keeping awake.

The van's only other occupant was its driver, Ray Hugger. Ray was a massive brute in his late twenties, well over six feet in height and powerfully built. One's first impression of him was that of lethargy. He always looked half-asleep, and the tuft of hair that persistently poked up from the back of his head did little to dispel this illusion. His strangely heavy eyes always seemed to be fighting a desperate battle with the sheer weight of their lids. He always reminded me of the village simpleton, who would be persuaded to climb into the ring to challenge the champion in country-fair boxing booths. Ray in fact belied his bovine appearance. He was an extremely intelligent man, who was also an outstanding goalkeeper, tennis player and sprinter. I could never really understand his ability to sprint; it seemed conjured out of nothing but sheer determination. He would come through on the last 40 yards of a 220-yard race with the ferocity of a demented bull. All in all, Ray was a very handy companion to have when searching warehouses in the dark!

Ray drove just a little like he would sprint – in a straight line and flat out. I was rather pleased that the distance between my entry to the police van and the warehouse location was three-quarters of a mile of dead straight road. It was an accepted fact at Wharf Road that Ray's driving was never suited to corners and bends. A few seconds later, he lifted his right foot from the floor, where it had been crushing the pulp out of the accelerator pedal. He then stamped it down with an equal ferocity on to the footbrake. My sitting position instantly changed from a forty-five-degree recline into a ninety-degree bow. The van juddered protestingly to a halt and I released my knuckle-whitening grip from the door handle. We had arrived.

There was one other police vehicle already on the scene, so we decided to spread the search. The warehouse alarm was of the silent type. This meant that the warning would go straight through to the telephone exchange. This in turn normally meant that any intruders would have been unaware of our presence. Silent alarm systems, however, did not cater for police vans that are driven like dumper trucks. We could therefore not afford to waste a second.

The crew of the other vehicle went immediately to the rear of the premises, while Ray and I decided to go straight to the roof. Access to this roof was not too difficult. An extremely thick wall, some two feet wide, ran at right angles to the warehouse and finally joined it at a point just a few feet beneath the rain gutter. It was then a comparatively simple task to pull oneself up over the edge. The main problem then lay in the delusive lure of the roof surface. We were extremely conversant with this fact, and our first task would be to look for the holes that had been left by others who were not.

The wall itself seemed to serve no useful purpose. It had obviously been a key part of some earlier structure that had been destroyed in the war. It ran for varying heights, beginning at almost roof-level at the warehouse, to just a few feet near the railway sidings some seventy yards away. It was towards these sidings that we both ran. We were soon on top of the wall and Ray picked his way swiftly along it with the confidence of a mountain goat. I was far more cautious, and I did not arrive at the roof until some time after my companion.

As I swung up over the guttering, I heard a shout from the other side of the roof. It seemed that Ray had already turned up something. I heard the sound of running footsteps but I could make out nothing in the darkness. My belated warning of 'Mind that roof!' was totally ignored by the runners. I gingerly picked my way towards the commotion, then I stopped still when I realized that the sound was now coming from away to my left. The chase, if this is what it was, was taking place around the perimeter. Well, that at least was the safest part of the roof. I very slowly turned and headed back for the wall, cursing myself for my stupidity in leaving it unguarded.

I could now see both figures clearly silhouetted against the street lights. Ray was in hot pursuit of Small Stan Tompkins and, even in that minefield of a surface, was gaining fast! I realized, probably even before Stan himself did, that if he were not to be caught by the closing copper, then he would have to jump. I also felt that was exactly what he would do. He did not falter for a second. He reached the junction of the roof and the wall, and simply leapt out into space, landing neatly in the centre of the wall some three feet below. He paused momentarily to assure himself of his balance, then legged it down the gradual decline to the distant sanctuary of the railway sidings. To my complete horror, Ray followed him!

The main difference between the two leaps was one of confidence. Stan's had been smooth and fluent, with never a doubt that he would make it. Ray's, on the other hand, though equally smooth, had been far more speculative. As a spectator I was quite sure that Stan would land safely; I was equally sure that Ray would miss. The amount of time that each spent in the air must have been about a tenth of a second. Yet Ray's jump was like a slow-motion trip to eternity.

He had in fact landed on both feet reasonably well but his body leaned to the right in a most alarming fashion. His arms went like windmills on the still night air and for a few long moments he appeared to teeter on the brink. Astonishingly enough, he regained his balance. I then expected to see him crouch down and clutch the top of the wall in grateful thanks. But no! The fool made off along the wall in hot pursuit of Stan.

'Leave him!' I yelled. 'And stand still! We can always pick him up later.'

If there were any question whether Ray should remain still, on grounds of safety, it was quickly dispelled by a sudden, deep rumbling. We both clearly heard the noise but Ray could not at first decipher its origin. I had no such problems.

'Run! The bloody wall is collapsing!'

The first two courses of bricks under his feet began to sink, as a whole section of the wall swayed ominously. A split second later, Ray gave the impression of being fired from a cannon. If he had been somewhat nonchalant in his ascent of the wall, his descent had all the hallmarks of blind terror. My warning yells, plus the cries from the crew who were searching the warehouse grounds, added strength to the feeling of imminent disaster.

Small Stan had by now reached the end of the wall. At that point he would normally have leapt to safety on to the railway embankment. But he stopped and watched in awed fascination as the galloping copper was pursued by the collapsing wall. Once Ray had reached the halfway stage, the first sizeable chunk of wall crumbled immediately behind him and crashed down to the yard some thirty feet below. Before there was any actual impact between the falling bricks and the ground, Ray put on a final despairing spurt. He certainly appeared to be moving much faster, but then so did the wall! Each time one of Ray's feet vacated the top course of bricks, so those bricks began to sink rapidly.

When Ray had almost reached the safety of the railway, I realized that at his present pace a collision between him and his now stationary quarry was inevitable. The knowledge of that particular fact seemed to dawn on Small Stan just a few seconds too late. He turned and vainly tried to jump the remaining few feet to safety. It seemed to me, however, that there was no way that Ray could now avoid him.

Just before the expected impact, Ray leapt from the wall on to the steep slopes of the railway embankment and totally vanished into the darkness. The last piece of wall then tumbled into a heap of rumbling dust, and when it finally cleared there was not a sign of either of the two runners.

The two searching policemen at ground level had meanwhile been joined by two more colleagues and all four now ran across the warehouse yard towards the overgrown embankment. The dark of the railway was too distant for any lights from the street lamps to penetrate. I could only stand powerless on the roof-edge and wait. I did not have to stand for too long, however. Two or three minutes after he had hurtled into the darkness, Ray Hugger limped slowly back through the long grass of the embankment and into the comparative clarity of the warehouse yard. He was alone, the other four coppers having taken off in futile pursuit of Small Stan.

'Are you all right, Ray?' I called down anxiously.

'Yeh, I'll be okay. Which is more than can be said for you!' came back the surprising reply.

'Me? Why? What d'you mean?' I asked, now with a great deal more than anxiety in my voice.

'Just *how* are you going to get down?'

I quickly looked around me with just a preliminary feeling of panic. I had not thought of that! I am not particularly good on roofs at the best of times. But on a fragile one with no means of escape – except through it – I could easily become hysterical.

It took only a few minutes to discover there was *no* other way down. By this time, more foot police had arrived and I was the object of a barrage of totally unhelpful remarks. The swift arrival of the fire brigade greatly assisted my peace of mind, but doubled my embarrassment. I finally made ground level with much help and no little trepidation.

'Don't worry about it, mate,' said the grinning fireman. 'We get more coppers down from roofs than cats from trees!'

I sighed with relief as finally I climbed into the police van.

'D'you think that kid'll be home yet?' asked Ray.

'Eh? Oh, Small Stan?' I had been so full of my own problems that I had completely forgotten about him. 'Yeh, he will just about have reached there by now. We'll call on our way back to the nick.'

A few minutes later, we shuddered to a halt outside Bridewell Dwellings. I wearily climbed to the third floor and knocked loudly on number 37.

Small Stan Tompkins emerged, dirt-stained and dusty.

''Allo, won't keep you a minute,' he said. 'Me dad's just putting 'is trousers on.'

A few seconds later we were joined by Stanley Henry Ian Tompkins senior.

''Allo, Mr Cole, ain't seen you fer a mumfth or two. 'Ow yer bin keepin', awlright?'

'Fine, thanks, Mr Tompkins, but Stan's been out thieving again,' I replied, with a sad shake of the head.

'Yeh, I know. 'E's bin tellin' me abaht it. Sounds really bleedin' terrifyin' ter me. I can't stand 'ights meself. D'yer wannus ter come dahn ter the nick, Mr Cole?'

'I should think that Mr Hugger would be more than delighted by that offer. Shall we go?'

'Sure. Come on, Stan-boy,' he sang out, cheerily. 'We're orf ter the nick.'

As always on these journeys to the station, neither father nor son would as much as mention the real reason for our little trip. They would dispute nothing, sign everything and plead guilty whenever the case came up in court.

Less than a month later, Arthur Mason, a local publican, awoke from an alcoholic slumber sometime around three in the morning. It was a stormy, windswept night. The footsteps that he believed had woken him were now silent. He crossed to the bedroom window and slightly parted the curtains. Many chimney pots and aerials were missing from their dripping moorings. Dustbins rolled back and forth; drain-pipes gurgled hungrily; and here and there a fence-gate banged. The night was so inhospitable that the very cold seemed to cocoon his fleshy body. He shuddered and returned to the sanctuary of his big warm bed, and Hilda, his big warm wife.

Forty feet below, Small Stan lay broken among the slates and pots, still clutching the frail aluminium aerial and its four loose screws.

'I thought it was only the good that died young?' said Ray Hugger to me, later that morning.

'Well, I think that maybe Stan *was* good,' I answered. 'He may never have run an errand for an aunt, but I feel that somehow he could just about have made "good".'

'Yes, p'raps you're right. Let's just say that he wasn't very good on roofs.'

The Cake 'As 'Ad a Miscarriage

'The trouble with the police force', said John Cain, my sociology teacher, 'is the insularity of its members.'

It was my second year at evening classes and I sat dozily in the large forty-seater classroom. Five other students sprawled equally inactive around the room.

The remark pierced my stupor. If ever there was a danger that the class might fall asleep, then John Cain considered the police force fair game. It was an obvious ploy but it always worked, probably because I never failed to bite. As a teacher, John knew this and considered it a legitimate weapon in his academic armoury. He would hurl controversial darts at no one else in the classroom. The bank cashier; the two English teachers; the pleasantly rounded mum and the unemployed homosexual cook, all were quite safe from his barbs. However should the eye of just one student close, then it was John Cain, versus Harry Cole and the Metropolitan Police Force.

'That's rubbish!' I exclaimed. 'Just how the hell do you arrive at that conclusion?'

The class began to stir. 'Rubbish', 'How the hell?': those words weren't sociological phrases, perhaps we were about to have a diversion?

'Well,' announced the tutor, quite pleased with the response he was now receiving from the awakening group. 'As a force, you live together, work together, socialize together and almost your entire life is led in the company of other policemen. Right?'

'Wrong! In fact you couldn't be more wrong!'

'Prove it.'

'Well, I live in a street of two hundred houses, with just three other coppers in it. I play football and cricket for a civvie club. I work in a boys' club that has nothing whatever to do with the police, and most of my friends are, in fact, outside the force.' That's destroyed him, I thought.

'Holidays? How about holidays?' he demanded, clutching at straws.

'I have never been on holiday with anyone other than my immediate family since I have been in the force,' I answered emphatically.

Life had returned to all six of us and John could now return to the topic from which he had so deliberately digressed.

'Okay, everyone,' he announced, 'let's get back to our subject – "The Theoretical Approach to the Methods of Sociology". Right, now, let us first take symbolic inter-action ...'

So the evening droned on. I never took John Cain's asides too seriously; it was a little like a game, really. He would hurl all the usual sociological theories at me and I would block them with equally predictable answers. Tonight, though, had been particularly pleasing. I could not think of one of his points which had struck home.

As I drove out of the school car park, I was not conscious that I was thinking about anything in particular. Suddenly a damning thought struck me. My daughter's holiday! John Cain was correct on that point. She was going to Paris in a couple of weeks and she was to stay with the family of a French policeman. Did that count? Well, I suppose it must. It was a holiday that had been arranged for some time. She was travelling by coach with numerous other coppers' kids. Later that year the visit would be

174

returned, by the daughter of the French policeman. The purpose of the holiday was not primarily one of recreation but of education. She would share a bedroom with her young Parisian girlfriend. She would also eat and converse in everyday French with the rest of the family. It was the first time she had been away from home for any length of time on her own. I had experienced some reservations; the first had been about the price.

'My French teacher at school said it would improve my "O" level exam chances no end, dad.'

'Oh yes? How much?'

'Er – it's really quite reasonable.'

'I'm sure it is. How much?'

'Well, it's ninety pounds actually, but that's all in.'

'If I'm paying ninety quid for seven days then I shall *feel* all in. I spent two years in the army for little more than that.'

'Oh come on,' said my wife. 'Ninety pounds to be able to speak fluent French does sound pretty reasonable to me.'

'Ninety pounds may sound pretty reasonable to you but it sounds bloody expensive to me.'

'Wouldn't you be proud of a daughter who spoke fluent French?' she persisted.

'There are times when I would be grateful enough if my daughter just spoke fluent English!' I realized that I was losing this argument and I grudgingly conceded.

'Subject to close supervision both of your safety and your language, then you can go. Agreed?'

'Agreed, dad.'

A cold wet Monday a few weeks later saw both Christine and me up at the crack of dawn. I drove her to New Cross where she was to catch a Paris-bound coach. This coach party consisted of forty-two girls of her own age on the same lease-lend trip, plus six supervising adults.

175

One week later, I waited on the same spot for the coach to return. It was, of course, two hours late. 'No matter,' I told myself, 'it will be well worth the delay. When she finally returns home, she will sound like Joan of Arc.'

Eventually the coach came into view. It was beribboned with tricolours and most of the girls sported berets. The French song that came from within was, coincidentally, the only one I've ever known: 'Aluetta, jaunty Aluetta!' Yes, there was no doubt about it, the trip had obviously been a good idea after all. Furthermore, I could not possibly see how this made me insular as a policeman. The fact that my daughter stayed with a gendarme was incidental. It would be the same if the fellow had been a road sweeper or a lorry driver. No, John Cain, you are not going to get through to me as easily as that this time.

An hour or so after meeting the coach, we were sitting around the fire drinking tea. We had soon begun to discuss the Paris trip in some detail.

'How's your French now?' I asked, trying to justify the ninety quid with whatever improvement there may have been in my daughter's linguistic ability.

'French?' she replied in some puzzlement. 'We didn't speak it once. There was no need to – everyone spoke English.'

I was stunned for a moment, then I exploded. 'Then what the hell was that week all about?'

'Dunno,' she said, matter-of-factly.

'You might just as well have spent the week at Clacton if you were speaking English all the time!' I pointed out. 'It would also have been considerably cheaper!'

'Didn't you do anything different?' asked my wife, hopefully. 'You couldn't go to Paris and not see *something* that you could not see in London, surely?'

'Oh yes, I remember!' exclaimed my daughter cheerfully. 'I saw my first "flasher"!'

'A flasher!? I paid nigh on a hundred quid for you to see a flasher? They are ten-a-penny in Greenwich Park in the summer. How about "O" levels, then? I realize they sit some pretty weird subjects in exams nowadays, but flashing? Surely not!'

'Oh come on, dad. Going to Paris was an experience for all of us girls. We were all in the same boat.'

'Forty-two girls at ninety quid a time is, by my reckoning, – let me see – three thousand and – bloody hell! Three thousand, seven hundred and eighty pounds and all you've got to show for it is one very cold exposed Frenchman! It's not languages you should be studying, it's bloody economics!'

It took me some weeks to overcome that little shock and it was fortunate that there was nearly four months before the visit was returned. The French girls were due to arrive at Victoria railway station late on a Thursday afternoon. Christine accompanied me and waited patiently at the barrier to claim our guest. Because the schools were now on holiday, she would be staying for fourteen days instead of seven. I studied the faces of each of the French children as they filed past the barrier. They looked no different from the faces of the English kids who were waiting to greet them. These youngsters, in turn, looked no different from every other child who happened to be in the precincts of the station. No, John Cain, I tell you, police families are not insular; or if they are, they certainly do not look it.

'There's Veronique, dad!' said Christine, excitedly.

A slightly built, pretty girl of average height smiled a greeting towards us.

"Ow do you do, Monsieur Cole?' she asked politely.

'Very well, thank you, Veronique. I'm sure you must be hungry, so we'll leave for home straight away.'

'Ah yes, hungry, I am very hungry indeed. It will be nice to be, er, un-hungry.'

177

If there was one thing that I learned during the next two weeks, it was that this kid could eat. She never stopped. The beauty of it was that she ate whatever was put down before her. She would then compliment whoever cooked it. An hour later, we reached home where my wife Joan was preparing the evening meal. The day was hot and the aroma drifted tantalizingly out of the open windows.

After greeting my wife as politely as she had me, Veronique exclaimed, 'Ah-ha. The dinner it is raining, yes?'

The three of us looked at one another and shrugged our shoulders. 'Yes,' we agreed. 'The dinner was absolutely pouring cats and dogs.'

Our assent seemed to please Veronique and she nodded her head. In fact, she continued to nod her head as she secured a place for herself at the dinner table.

'Veronique,' said Joan, 'would you care for a wash before dinner?'

She ceased nodding her head and began to shake it vigorously. 'Non!' she exclaimed.

That was our first indication of the girl's total abhorrence of soap and water.

I had arranged three days' leave so the four of us made the usual tourist rounds of London. As those few July days slipped by, the presence of Veronique became more and more powerful. Her daily ablutions consisted of three long brushings of her teeth and three generous sprays of perfume.

'Her toothbrush smells great,' said Joan ruefully. 'I only wish she did!'

The sixth day of her stay began hot and sunny. I left for work very early that morning. I was on duty in The Mall for a state visit by a foreign dignitary. The two girls later decided to set out to find and surprise me. Shortly before noon, while directing some Americans to Grosvenor Square, a now familiar scent assailed my nostrils. I felt a tap on the shoulder and turned to see both girls standing behind me.

'We 'ave found you, Monsieur Cole,' beamed Veronique, delighted.

'I was aware of it, luv, I was most certainly aware of it.'

On arriving home that evening, I said to Joan, 'We've got to do something about that kid, or we'll have the sanitary inspector around here.'

'Well, I've tried persuasion,' she protested. 'Short of actually hauling her bodily into a hot bath, I cannot see what more we can do.'

'Well, on Friday evening we are all going to the Royal Tournament at Earls Court. If she doesn't bathe before then, well, she's just not going. I bet it's bloody months since that kid's body has hit water!'

'I've an idea!' said Joan suddenly. 'How about if we all dress up posh-like for the Tournament? Veronique has very few clothes with her, so I can tell her that she can wear one of Christine's long dresses on condition that she has a bath!'

We decided to give the idea a run – and it worked perfectly! More than that, the girl looked absolutely beautiful. Beneath that 'BO' exterior had been a lovely young woman trying to get out. Indeed, the purification had arrived in the nick of time because Friday had dawned hot and very, very humid; so humid, in fact, that I was already having misgivings about dressing up 'posh-like'.

'We must go through with it,' said Joan nobly. 'A promise is a promise, particularly to a child.'

Feeling wildly conspicuous – most of the audience were clad in jeans and tee shirts – the four of us took our seats. The show was excellent, the last event being a huge set-piece with bands, horses and soldiers acting out Napoleon's retreat from Moscow. Now, as most readers will no doubt realize, Napoleon did not emerge from that little adventure any too well. However, the spectacle seemed to fire Veronique's patriotic fervour to an extreme, because she accompanied the brass band in a spirited rendition of the *Marseillaise*. She not only sang it during the performance, she continued singing it in the car park after the pageant had ended.

I have always considered myself quite a tolerant person, but twenty minutes of unrelenting, soul-stirring French chauvinism was beginning to strain my *entente cordiale*.

'Don't you know any English songs, Veronique?' I pleaded.

'I know "White Christmas",' came the astonishing reply.

With that, she burst into song and, having obviously learnt it parrot-fashion, proceeded to render all four verses. We were by this time driving along the Chelsea embankment. I suppose just to humour the child, we all joined in. I stopped the car beside a number 39 bus while waiting for the traffic lights to change. The West Indian bus driver must have thought he was receiving a heavenly message.

'. . . Just like the ones I used to know . . .'

He put his head out of the cab and looked all around him. He failed to see (like all bus drivers!) the car that was immediately beneath him, with its windows wide open.

'. . . Where the tree-tops glisten . . .'

He looked behind him into the bus.

'. . . To hear the sleigh bells in the snow . . .'

The traffic lights changed to green, the temperature remained at eighty degrees and we pulled away from the stop-line. The bus did not move. Veronique was extremely reluctant to let the song go. Her father had the record by Bing Crosby and she had learned it at a very early age.

'Again!' she cried, as four parched throats concluded: '. . . And may all your Christmases be white.'

That evening I discovered that it was possible to sing 'White Christmas' seven times between Earls Court and Chelsea Bridge before you actually go mad.

If Veronique was any guide, the French took the loss of Algeria more easily than any imagined slight to their singing. In an effort to break the monopoly of 'White Christmas', I hummed the opening bars of the *Marseillaise*. Again it worked like a charm. She switched tunes immediately and remained with it until she fell exhausted into bed an hour later.

On the following day, I was late-turn, and therefore at home in the morning. Summer appeared to have had its fling and a chill drizzle swept across south London. My wife suggested that the girls might care to stay indoors and attempt some cooking. (Anything was better than that infernal *Marseillaise*.) In time, with a little international goodwill, a rather dubious-looking cake had been mixed by both girls. I had taken more than a passing interest in its preparation, mainly because I was expected to take a generous slice of it to work. I had my first doubts when I saw that all the fruit had sunk to the bottom of the cake.

'I don't think that is quite right, Veronique,' I ventured.

'Ah-ha, monsieur, the bottom half is for people who like fruit cake and the top half is for...'

'Yes, yes, I know. People who like plain cake?' I interrupted. With a sales-line like that, I thought, no wonder the French are running the Common Market.

This segregation of ingredients was not the only fault to appear. The area in the middle of the cake had the appearance of a small swamp. The girls then decided to tell each other in their partner's language exactly where the fault lay. Christine made her attempt in French and, not being acquainted with the language, I could only assume that she was successful. Veronique, on the other hand, was a subscriber to the 'if-a-job's-worth-doing-it's-worth-doing-well' school of thought. Collecting her French-English dictionary, she perused it for some ten minutes. She closed it thoughtfully, looked up and smiled.

'Monsieur!' she announced grandly. 'The cake 'as 'ad a miscarriage.'

Now I am neither a cook nor a linguist, but I well understood the message.

Eventually, after some forty-seven versions of the *Marseillaise* and a similar number of 'White Christmas's, the two weeks came to an end. The purpose of those exchanges is for the children to broaden their outlook, in the hope that everyone will learn something. From that viewpoint, the visit was a great success. Christine improved her French; Veronique improved her English *and* her hygiene; my wife learnt all the verses of 'White Christmas', and I shall never eat another cake.

Most of the credit goes to the child, of course. Any French kid who eats bangers and beans, pie and mash, fish and chips, porridge and bread pudding will obviously be a delight to cater for.

I have just one gnawing misgiving. Just what did this visit do for my law-enforcing insularity?

Thief-takers

The 3 a.m. night bus throbbed its way past me along the deserted Walworth Road. I looked up without any great interest. I was walking a set patrol that was very limited in its area: it incorporated about 600 yards of main-road shops, plus a few alleys that gave access to the rear of many of these premises. A cheery 'What ho!' caused me to pause and turn around. 'Bimbo' Ronson had emerged from one of these alleys and was increasing his stride to join me. I groaned inwardly.

Bimbo had been a copper for exactly six months and already his disasters were legendary. It had been a source of wonder to the rest of the station, how he had managed to pass the interview board in the first place. However, we had recently heard on the grapevine that Bimbo's days in the force were now numbered.

All police recruits have to complete a two-year probationary period. During this time they are regularly reported on by a sergeant and an inspector, the idea being to assure their competence in all aspects of police work. It was this form of intermediary check that was about to be Bimbo's undoing.

Bimbo, alias 'The Skreaming Skull' alias 'Bones' and just occasionally Dennis, should never in any way have measured up to any police standard. If his academic background was scant, his physical appearance was astonishing. No matter what the season, he always appeared to be in the final stages of consumption. I once heard a colleague claim that before

Bimbo reached the age of twenty-three he would have died of senility.

That night Bimbo had been posted to numbers one and two beats. These beats neatly circuited my patrol. The result of this posting meant that I could not really lose him. We sauntered along the main road, glancing from time to time into the shop windows. Just occasionally we would notice a change of display from the previous night. We would pass an opinion on the merits of these displays and walk on.

After a few minutes, I was vaguely aware of a small car approaching from the direction of the Elephant and Castle. While the speed of this car was by no means excessive, it most certainly was not hanging about. Apart from the bus, it was the first vehicle we had seen for some fifteen minutes and as such it attracted Bimbo's attention. As the car neared the traffic lights at the junction just ahead of us, I heard the familiar roar of a newspaper delivery van. These high-backed, four-wheeled vans hurtled around London in the early hours, pausing only to throw out great bundles at newspaper shops. The van, which was now approaching from a side street, struck the rubber pad that activates the traffic lights. There is a three-second 'all red' safety phase at this junction and once the pad is struck the whole electronic cycle clicks into an irreversible sequence.

The small car had just reached the point of 'no return' when the traffic lights changed against it. There was instantly an increase in the car's speed and it crossed the junction on rather a late amber. Not, perhaps, an advisable thing to do but similarly not the world's greatest crime. I momentarily took in the whole situation and dismissed it as of no great consequence. I then returned my gaze to the shop windows. There I inspected with some interest

184

a set of red satin lingerie that had not been on show the previous night.

'Did you see that? He went through the amber!' exclaimed Bimbo. 'I'm gonna stop him!'

Before I could make a move to prevent him, he raised his right hand and stepped straight into the path of the oncoming car. At that moment I was absolutely convinced that Bimbo would never live long enough to reach his premature senility. On the other hand, the car driver had not abandoned all hope and he made a successful attempt to avoid a justifiable homicide. He swerved the car sharply and braked at the same time – a disastrous combination. The speeding vehicle tilted frighteningly at a forty-five-degree angle and appeared to run for some distance on two wheels. It then turned completely on its side and continued in a shower of sparks for another thirty-five yards.

I looked at the whole scene in disbelief. The car had ground to a final halt on its side on the opposite pavement, its front wheels still turning merrily. Bimbo looked around over his shoulder with his mouth agape, his hand still raised. The newspaper van had emerged from the side street and accelerated away towards the Elephant and Castle just as if nothing had happened. The most maddening aspect was that if Bimbo had showed the same interest in ladies' red satin underwear as I had shown, nothing would have happened!

I raced across the road to the overturned car, fully aware of the ominous smell of petrol. The passenger door, which was now in the same position as a sunshine roof, was thrown back like the hatch of a submarine. A thick-set, balding man struggled to free himself from the interior. I assisted him clear and we both backed quickly away. The engine had by this time stalled and the wheels had ceased to spin.

There were a few crackles and rattling noises but within a couple of minutes everything else seemed quiet.

'Phew!' panted the driver. 'I was bloody lucky there!'

'I think we might just be able to push it upright,' I said. 'Come on, we'll give it a try.'

'Leave it where it is,' exclaimed Bimbo, who had by now finally made the journey across the road. 'It's evidence. I'm going to summons him for a traffic-light offence.'

I was rapidly losing my patience with my fellow officer.

'Don't be a prat! We can't leave it there! There's petrol leaking everywhere. Give us a shove, you idiot, and we'll stand it up!'

Bimbo reluctantly joined the driver and me, and after a couple of attempts we rocked it back to an upright position.

'I'll just try my ignition,' said the driver.

He switched on and I was astonished to hear the engine start first time. I was looking into the car from the driver's side when Bimbo appeared on the opposite side and opened the passenger door. Now I must say, at this stage, that I thought the car driver had been most sporting about the whole situation. I know that if I had been in his position I would have felt close to murder. I had doubted, in fact, that Bimbo would survive for more than two seconds after his suicidal hand signal.

'Why are you in possession of three chequebooks, sir?' asked Bimbo, more puzzled than suspicious.

The driver appeared more agitated by the question than by the crash.

'Oh – er, yes, they belong to members of my family,' he faltered.

'But they are in three different names, sir?' queried Bimbo, suspicion now gaining.

'Yes, they are my in-laws.'

'Don't happen to know their names, do you, sir?'

186

'Er – no, you see I've only recently married.'

'You mean to say you don't know who you've married?' I asked incredulously.

Bimbo opened the glove compartment and another six chequebooks fell out into his lap.

'Do you work in a bank, sir?'

The driver closed his eyes and placed his head on the backs of his hands, which were in turn hanging from the top of the steering wheel.

I took the precaution of switching off the engine and removing the ignition keys.

'I'm an unlucky bastard, I am!' he almost sobbed.

He was certainly correct there. David Walter Baxter was wanted by half the police forces in the north of England. The car was stolen and had been false-plated. In the boot were the proceeds from three burglaries, together with a further eight chequebooks. Five fur coats lay between the front and rear seats, each of them carefully wrapped around some rather exclusive-looking silverware.

'The Skreaming Skull' had struck again! Dennis Bimbo Ronson had just emerged from a move which, had anyone else attempted it, would probably have resulted in the deaths of two people. That vehicle should by rights have killed either him or its driver – and yet it didn't. The suspect in the car was a first-class villain who subsequently went away for five years.

This was by no means the first time Bimbo had struck during his short stay at Wharf Road. The fact that he had an unquestionable flair for catching crooks could not be denied. He could not explain how or why he accomplished it, yet virtually every time that boy walked out of the station, so he would return with a big villain.

Within a month of David Baxter's arrest, the police force and Bimbo had parted company. No one at Wharf Road was surprised – except by the fact that it had taken so long to happen. In spite of all his faults, Bimbo was that very rare animal – a great thief-taker.

Not all thief-catchers are dispensed with as swiftly and as easily as Bimbo. Many of them soldier on for years. But in the vast majority of cases, they all acquire one thing in common: they rarely stay the full course. In fact it would be more accurate to say they have *two* things in common, for they also provide the backs that carry the rest of us along.

None did this more than PC James Cave.

If Bimbo's parting was inevitable, then Jimmy Cave's was tragic. Jim was the epitome of all thief-catchers and he caught them non-stop for seventeen years. Bimbo's swansong was an overturned car at three in the morning in the deserted Walworth Road. Jim's was a Miss World contest that was screened to half the television sets around the world. Bimbo caught villains and never knew why he caught them. Jim caught them because that was his job and he knew he was good at it. When Bimbo remembers his days in the force, he thinks no doubt of Walworth Road and Camberwell. Jim remembers the Albert Hall and how it all went wrong for him there.

Jim Cave, a Liverpudlian, was a powerful, fearless type of individual who, in his early days in particular, was very much a rough diamond. For eight years he had been a regular soldier in the Brigade of Guards, serving, among other places, in Palestine and Tripoli. On joining the Metropolitan Police he discovered his amazing flair for catching thieves. Unlike Bimbo, he would not leave the station and collide with them, Jim would smell them out. Then, having smelt them out, he would attack them with all guns blazing. Whilst Jim's overall total will never be known, in the last two years of his service alone he made 163 crime arrests! These offences were not for bus lane infringements, dogs without rear lights, or drunk and refusing to fight. They were for genuine, 100 per cent crime. During his seventeen years in the force, he received no fewer than thirteen commendations, including two by the commissioner. While he served he was brave, unshakeable and dedicated; when he left he was sad, disillusioned and bitter.

The police force itself has a great deal to recommend it. It has a camaraderie and humour unrivalled in any other field. Sadly, it has also its Jim Caves. One of the great problems for any force is the difficulty it must experience in handling such people. It will never be an easy task. One sure thing about the truly great thief-takers is that they are not easy to handle. They are likely to make so many waves that the superintendent's desk could become awash with complaints. Superintendents as a general rule do not care for this. After serving his statutory first two years in uniform, Jim applied to work in the Criminal Investigation Department. He was quickly accepted and became a plain-clothes 'aide'. Aides were the general dogsbodies of the CID. They would be responsible for a great deal of the boring routine work, such as observations and house-to-house enquiries. At the end of a period, usually six months, their services would be either extended or dispensed with, according to their record. They would work in pairs, ideally a younger aide with an older one. These six-month periods could be prolonged and many men were aides for several years. Provided an aide was considered suitable material for the department, he would eventually emerge into a fully fledged detective. To accomplish this he would first need to pass the grade one civil service exam, and subsequently a selection board. Jim never got past the exam! Seven times he sat that exam and seven times he failed. The years rolled by and Jim remained an aide while several of his partners soared to higher things, many of them as a result of what they had learnt from Jim.

As one detective inspector once told him in a fit of exasperation: 'How can you ever hope to become a good detective if you can't square a pi and don't know what grows on the left bank of the river Zambezi?'

It was the day after failing one of these exams that Jim drove down the Camberwell Road in his old Standard Eight motor car. I used to believe that car had its own gravity field. I found it impossible to understand how the numerous loose parts would otherwise stay in place. The noise from each moving part – and also from those which were not supposed to move – rendered his car horn obsolete. The purpose of the drive was to call in at a Camberwell toy shop. It was approaching Christmas and Jim and his fellow aide, 'Buck' Rogers, were about to begin their shopping. Little did they realize the bag they were to make.

Walking in the same direction as Jim were four men. This quartet was attempting nothing suspicious, they were simply strolling along the pavement and chatting together. Yet just as soon as Jim's eyes alighted upon them he stopped the car.

'You follow them on foot,' he said to his partner, 'and I'll stay further behind in the car.'

'Yes – but why?' came the understandable reply.

'I don't know, but there's something wrong with them. They look like four bloody good villains to me!'

Now that is hardly a cast-iron case for any prosecution to present to a court. 'Mr Cave thought that the defendants all looked like "four bloody good villains", m'lud.'

Buck was quite used to Jim's inspired guesses, but even he had doubts as he trundled along behind the chattering four. The whole party soon reached the junction of Camberwell Green. Here the four men boarded a bus and climbed the stairs to the top deck. Buck slipped into a seat just inside the bus and therefore could not hear the suspects' requested destination. Jim by now had decided to question the four men. He accelerated past the bus and called in at Peckham police station, in order to request some uniformed assistance in stopping the vehicle.

Whether at this stage the suspects had become suspicious or whether they were simply nearing their destination, no one ever knew. Whatever the reason, they suddenly clambered down the stairs on to the platform. From here they could see the crew of a police car signalling the bus driver to stop, so they swiftly leapt from the still-moving bus and fled. They scattered in all directions and a chase ensued. The half-a-dozen coppers now taking part had no idea why or whom they were chasing. Three of the men were soon captured although one escaped. On checking the identities of the three men at the station, each was discovered to be wanted and no fewer than forty robberies were cleared up.

Whatever makes one person think that another person looks a 'bloody good villain'? If it had been me, I would probably have bid them good morning and walked on. There were many things that separated Jim from the average copper. No detail would be too small for him to follow up. He would frequent all shops or premises that dealt with the buying or selling of second-hand goods. He would spend hours in the vicinity and scrutinize everyone entering or leaving. His haul would be amazing. The medium-sized man wearing a large-size jacket near the pawn shop at Camberwell Green was typical.

'Whose jacket are y'wearing, mate?' asked Jim.

'Mine.'

'It don't fit you.'

'It was a present.'

'It's too big!'

'It was a present, I tell you.'

'You wear a jacket that's too big because it's a present?'

'Yes.'

'I don't believe you. I think you nicked it.'

'On my mother's life I didn't.'

'On my mother's life you did.'

There was a half minute's pause while the man in the jacket considered all of his options.

'Well, I didn't actually nick it. The car window was wide open and it was lying on the back seat. I would have said that it was more like me finding it, than nicking it.'

'No, I would say it's more like you nicking it,' corrected Jim.

'Well, I think that's bloody unfair.'

'I thought you might. Look, sunshine, you've nicked a jacket and I've nicked you. There surely can't be anything unfair about that. I would have said that it was extremely fair, wouldn't you?'

Faced with Jim's brand of logic, our villain could only murmur, 'I s'pose it is, really.'

'Well, there you are, then,' explained Jim. 'If you go around taking stuff that don't belong to you, then a big bad policeman is going to take you away. You ought to know that, it's in all the books. Right?'

'Right,' agreed the villain.

The England rugby captain who had carelessly left his leather jacket lying inside his open-windowed car was indeed a fortunate man that day.

Jim was also a great exponent of the now obsolete 'sus' law. This law, which became a political football, was used by him to great effect in the early 1960s. The 'sus' law, or to give it its legal definition, 'Being a suspected person loitering with the intent to commit a felony', was indeed a lethal weapon for him. As more and more people owned motor cars, so the habit of driving to the cinema grew. Cars were rarely parked on the main roads in those days and therefore the dingy side-turnings in the vicinity of cinemas became a thieves' paradise.

Medlar Street, Camberwell, was one such example. It was

quiet, with few residential properties; it was dark and it was alongside the Regal cinema. Jim and yet another of his partners, one Bill Swann, decided to have a look at the situation. Bill perched himself with a torch on a low roof, halfway down the street. Jim, meanwhile, hung around the front of the cinema. If anyone who wandered down Medlar Street looked in any way suspicious, then Bill would flash the torch once. This action was purely a warning. A second flash, however, would indicate that the suspect was now actually tampering with a vehicle. This would also be the signal for Jim to investigate.

On these occasions, Jim would use any local cover that might be available. Usually this would take the form of a passer-by, simply walking down the street. Jim would join them and chatter inanely away, often to their great consternation.

On one particular occasion, a tall, slim, attractive woman left the cinema and turned into Medlar Street. Jim quickly caught up with her and, to allay her fears, he showed her his warrant card and explained his mission. She was extremely co-operative and chatted away excitedly as they neared the suspect, who was by now inside a car and removing the radio. In the gloom of the street, all that could be clearly seen was the open car door and two feet. Jim suddenly left his companion and quickly pounced. It was an absolute bang-to-rights job. The wires were hanging loose from the dashboard and the thief had a screwdriver in one hand and the car radio in the other.

"'Ere! Whatta you doing with my husband?' demanded the woman of Jim.

'Whatta you doin' with my missus?' demanded the thief.

'Whatta *you* doin' in this bloody car?' demanded Jim.

The husband was as quiet as a lamb but the wife now become a tigress. It took the swift arrival of Bill Swann to pacify her. The couple had apparently arranged to meet outside the cinema but the contents of the unattended car had proved to be too much of a distraction for him.

Jim had long ago left the routine work of most aides far behind. He worked on numerous robberies and a family-feud shooting. In the meantime he continued regularly to fail his civil service exams. After his seventh attempt, he was sent for by the detective inspector.

'I'm sorry, Jim, but the rules have changed. The force now believes that if you haven't made detective after seven years, you are never going to make it. I will have to have you returned to uniform.'

So ended the plain-clothed career of temporary detective Cave.

For Jim this was indeed a blow. He needed the adrenalin induced by nicking villains. The more mundane side of police work – accidents, disturbances, disputes and patrolling – was not for him. London was full of crime and he needed to be amongst it, sorting it out and feeling collars.

There was now no way that he could ever become a detective, so he applied to become a dog-handler. To the force's credit, he was soon allocated a dog. It had the unbelievable name of Xumac – pronounced Shumac. If he was successful as a detective, as a dog-handler he was phenomenal. His experience as an aide was, of course, a help; but most of all it was his pure animal instinct for catching thieves that saw him through.

Having chased a burglar at a distance across a park one cold January night, he lost him in some bushes. The dog searched the undergrowth thoroughly but without success. There was a small public toilet nearby that afforded the only other cover. The door was not locked and Jim and Xumac soon ascertained that the place was empty. He was about to leave when he realized that he had not searched the small attic that housed the water supply tank. He wriggled his way into the tiny alcove but it was as empty as the toilet had been. He dropped back down to the floor and was about to give the dog a free rein to search the rest of the park. On a sudden impulse he decided to return to the alcove. He opened the flap – again, nothing. He placed his hand into the still, dark waters of the tank, and a wriggling half-frozen body met his touch! The burglar had stepped into the tank of water with an outside temperature around freezing – and he had submerged himself! Before the unfortunate fellow could be charged with 'breaking and entering', he had to be treated at Guy's Hospital for exposure!

Jim and his dog literally were a force in themselves. I do not know the record for arrests by one single officer on any one occasion, but the eleven that Jim arrested one night must be pretty high on that list. For a change, the offences were not for crime but for gaming in the street, although I would strongly suspect that the primary offence was under the 'being-rude-to-Jim-Act'.

The men, all in their late teens and early twenties, had recently emerged from a nearby public house. On the pavement outside, they had begun a noisy game of pitch-and-toss. Jim had been sent to the scene in response to complaints and the lads had all given him a torrent of abuse. Now purely on appearance alone, one did not abuse Jim. But not only had Jim been abused but so had his dog! Jim frequently referred to this animal as 'son' and there were occasions when it was easy to see why. The result of this little confrontation was eleven young men lined up in the charge room at Wharf Road.

Now one of the busiest people at any police station is the station officer. He is responsible for practically everything that could, should or ought to happen in the building. Any prisoner taken into the charge room can be a serious distraction from a station officer's work, but eleven at one time will be a nightmare! The quick glance that he gave the clock was not so much for the official entry on the charge sheet but more a mental calculation as to the time he was likely to arrive home for bed.

Jim gave the brief facts concerning the evidence. He also produced some coins and a few cards that had been used in the gaming. It was while this property was being listed that he took something from his pocket and planted an object among the prisoners' property. It was an article that he had been carrying around for weeks, waiting for an opportunity like this to arise.

'Oh, sergeant,' said Jim, matter-of-factly, 'we had a little skirmish in the street and my dog bit him.' He pointed to a spotty youth with the longest hair in the room. 'Well, I don't really know how to say this, but, well, Xumac has bit the prisoner's ear off,' he finally blurted out.

So saying, Jim slid a bloodstained *plastic* ear across the table towards the sergeant. Eleven prisoners was bad enough, but one minus an ear through the playfulness of a police dog is absolutely calamitous. The effect lost nothing by the actions of the puzzled youth. He placed an enquiring hand into his greasy locks and stood there looking extremely vacant. The station officer's recovery was gradual but within a couple of hours he was taking nourishment. However he never forgave Jim for the rest of his service. It was soon after the incident with the ear that Jim was to have a meeting that would change his entire life.

Through carrying out some routine police work, he chanced to meet Eric Morley, then head of the Mecca Group, and his wife Julia, who were together responsible for the annual Miss World contest. After several meetings, the conversation understandably turned to that particular year's competition. During the two weeks that led up to the evening finals, security was obviously a risk. The 'Women's Lib' and the 'Angry Brigade' had each made their protests at these televized events. Because of this risk, it was the habit of the organizers to take on extra staff for this period. Would Jim be interested? Very much so!

Policemen at that time were about as poor as church mice. The low pay rates had made it simply impossible for some men with young families to make ends meet on police pay. In my own case, two or three of the youngsters who attended my youth club earned more money for one night's work on a Sunday newspaper than I earned in a whole week of driving a police car in one of the toughest areas of London.

Nevertheless, in agreeing to help out at the Miss World contest, Jim was taking a calculated risk. The police discipline code states very clearly that members of the force must devote their whole time to police service. There is no special provision made for running around the town with the world's most beautiful women. It was very sticky ground, and Jim knew it. The obvious defence to any allegation of contravening the code would be to claim that no payment was ever made. There were, after all, many perks to the job. The welfare of the girls was an example. Even though each girl was allocated her own female chaperon, wherever they went, Jim went. It was to be a whole new world for the Wharf Road policeman. Each November he would be required to take three weeks' annual leave and begin his heady round of London's high society. The problem he faced, however, was that should the news of his annual job leak out, he might not be able to persuade the force to believe that he had received no payment. I thought he would not. Jim, ever the optimist, thought differently and accepted the offer.

The responsibility of the job was quite great. One evening at the Waldorf Hotel, the sixth-floor haven of the young ladies was placed under virtual siege by a dozen members of the Southern Counties rugby team who were residing on the floor below. The small Mecca squad quickly realized that they were losing the battle with these athletic giants. Suddenly Jim noticed a Guards tie around the neck of the largest of the attackers. He quickly appealed – as a former Guardsman – to his adversary's sense of fair play. The assailant then promptly changed sides!

It was around the time that Jim was beginning his annual work for Mecca that a great irony arose. With superb timing, the force abolished the need for budding detectives to pass the civil service exam. Unfortunately for Jim, it was the perfect Catch-22 situation, for he was now considered too old to re-enter the department. It was almost as if the rule had finally served its purpose and could now safely be repealed. Jim had slowly come to terms with the fact that he was never going to become a detective. To his credit, he threw himself into his new role of dog-handler with a zeal that made him one of the finest in the force. It was to avail him little.

In the autumn of 1970, Jim as usual submitted his annual leave application to cover the weeks of that year's beauty competition. He expected no problems, it was practically a formality. Much to his astonishment, the application was refused, with no reason offered. There were only two other Wharf Road men on leave at that time, both for very short periods. This was also a very quiet time of the year. The refusal could only mean one thing – someone, somewhere, had smelt a rat.

Jim immediately queried the reason and was told that he could take his leave at any period that he wished – except November! No matter how many questions he asked, still no one would give him an answer. It was now obvious to all, however, that the authorities not only knew of his part in the annual contest, but were determined to stop him playing at it. Not satisfied with the responses, or lack of them, that he received from his superintendent, he applied to see the commissioner. This is a little like the parish priest requesting to see the pope. Every constable is given the right to apply; whether or not he ever actually sees him or not is a different matter. Jim was a 'different matter'.

There is no doubt that in his frustration, Jim was beginning to make waves. His determination to see the commissioner was probably the greatest of these. He had been on sticky ground throughout his association with the Miss World contest and his friends knew it. While we admired his ability to bridge the enormous gap between being a Wharf Road copper and his role in an international competition, we nevertheless worried for him. Up until that moment we had all been fairly neutral in the dispute. After all, Jim was an adult and experienced copper who had entered into this arrangement with his eyes open. He had taken a calculated risk and it looked as if it was about to backfire on him. So be it, we thought, those are the rules of the game. If you break these rules, then you must expect a free kick to be awarded against you. Well, a free kick was most certainly awarded but it was awarded with such a pettiness that the force alienated the feeling of almost every Wharf Road officer, friend of Jim's or otherwise.

Four days before the competition was due to take place, Jim was informed that from that date he would cease to be a dog-handler. He would now report for duty on the shifts and in fact for the rest of that week he would be driving a panda car. I felt it was a bit like kicking the milkman's horse. This was the worst possible news for him. Jim and Xumac were not just a team, they were a whole bloody inseparable force! In this way nobody won. It must have been apparent to whoever drafted that punishment that Jim would never be able to accept it. For a start, the dog would be completely wasted; it was now much too old to be re-trained for a new handler.

Jim himself would obviously lose: he had lived for the job, sniffing out villains like a sanitary inspector around

199

a broken drain. The force would lose: its rare breed of thief-takers would be diminished greatly by this one blow. And how about us, his colleagues? We would lose. It was as if the cornerstone of the whole structure of crime-fighting in Walworth had been demolished, together with our morale. More than anyone, the public would lose. Without Jim and his dog, the streets would be just that bit more uncertain to walk.

Jim was then served with notice that discipline proceedings were to be taken against him. We all thought that this was little more than a formality. If he did not get his dog back then the proceedings would be pointless because he would not be in the force long enough to face them. Jim had in fact decided differently. He would cling on until the enquiry, in the hope of retrieving Xumac. It was, of course, not to be.

At the subsequent discipline hearing Jim's pay was reduced for a year. Jim resigned the day after the hearing and left the force after seventeen years, a sad and bitter man.

It could be said that some of Jim's misfortunes were self-inflicted. I would not quarrel with that premise. But I do sometimes marvel at the force's inability to cope with its Jim Caves. They are special men and they require special handling. With so many courses and man-management studies available, it seems that sometimes we still cannot handle them.

I once asked Jim if there was a secret in catching crooks. Did the dog, for example, give him an advantage over equally dedicated police officers?

'No,' he replied. 'It doesn't really matter if you've got a dog or a camel; if you're a thief-catcher, then you'll catch thieves.'

On Jim's last count, eight of the partners who had served with him went on to the ranks of detective inspector or above. One, in fact, reached the heady heights of chief constable. It may well be that each of these men would have managed equally well under his own steam. On the other hand, they had two things going for them: they had Jim as a partner and a pretty fair knowledge of the geography of the Zambezi.

There was a happy footnote to this story. Xumac was indeed too old to re-train as a police dog. In order to prevent the animal from being put down, Jim managed to acquire the creature and he re-trained it as a pet for the last few years of its life.

The Vandal?

That high, corrugated-iron fencing had finally been removed from around the new council estate, reminding me of a stripper who has taken off her final cloak. There it was at last, bared for all to see. I stood for some minutes and studied each section intently. I slowly became lost in admiration – this was more like it! Had they finally got it right? Only time would tell, of course, but for the very first time I was optimistic.

The environment of the area had been founded on tightly knit houses, alleys and courtyards. Now it appeared that the wheel had finally completed its full circuit. We had travelled via the old slums and the new high-rise flats and it looked as though we had arrived back exactly where we had begun, five hundred years ago. This fifteen-year, expensive flirtation with skyscraper blocks had been a ruinous disaster. No one except eagles should have to raise offspring 300 feet above the ground.

I stepped through the fence-posts and wandered around the estate. I could hardly believe it. This really had to be right, it was a last throw and it had to succeed. It would depend, of course, entirely on the residents, but if this place was to be turned into a slum in a few years' time, then we all should really begin to despair. Most of the houses were just little terraced cottages, with gravel paths and small gardens front and rear. The estate contained some two hundred dwellings and the borders extended to link up with two other similar and recently completed estates. This was probably its main weakness. A little isolation would not have come amiss.

The elderly folk were catered for in the somewhat grandly named 'Lawn Court'. This was a small area of terraced houses where they were provided with either large bed-sits or one-bedroom flats. An illuminated sign was installed above each exterior door which would be switched on by the occupier in times of trouble. It flashed the solitary word 'HELP'.

It was too much to expect that everything would be perfect, of course. The council had omitted to recruit any caretakers for the estate and rubbish was already accumulating. More important, the architects had yet again followed their fanatic belief that elderly people worship the sounds of playing children. The large family units were therefore predictably next to the old people's flats. In spite of this, as the local copper I hoped that the sheer design of the estate would help the residents become more community-minded. This in turn could alleviate much of the conflict between the young and the old. Communication between the factions was always half of the battle anyway.

As the next few weeks slipped by, I watched with interest as the families began to move in. It was spring and I was astonished how many of the tenants began work immediately on their gardens. The vast majority of them had never possessed so much as a pot of daffs. In spite of this, their efforts to transform six square yards of heavy London clay into a riot of colour were astonishingly successful. I selfishly thought that here at last was a housing estate that would never be a problem for me. I was wrong yet again.

A month later, I had just begun a 2 p.m. to 10 p.m. tour of duty. I was about to leave the station when I was captured by Sergeant Peter Cage.

'Ah, Cole! You've been to evening classes, haven't you?' he asked, casually.

'Yes,' I agreed, with probably just a hint of suspicion in my voice.

'I wondered if you would like to do a very important liaising job for me? I think it calls for a chap like you. You would have to meet some local academic representatives.'

'Just what do you mean by "liaising"? And what are "academic representatives"? They sound like a right bloody lumber to me.'

He sighed. 'Why are you always prepared to believe the worst of me? It is very hurtful, you know. All I require you to do is to go along and impress a group of local teachers with your awe-inspiring presence. Now that's not much to ask, is it?'

'All right! All right! I'll go! Now will you just tell me what it is that I have let myself in for? And where is it that I am to give this talk?'

'Talk? It's not a talk. Nothing as difficult as a talk. All I want you to do is to go down to the old town hall at 2.30 p.m. and join seven other equally gifted constables. There you will see one hundred and fifty local teachers. They are going to demonstrate by marching to the education offices in Peckham, two miles away. They are protesting about the cuts in the education programme. You know how these marchers always like someone to talk to – it helps them pass the time and they don't notice the distance.'

'Bloody hell, sergeant, have you looked out of the window? It's bucketing down with rain!'

'Oh, that's all right, I think they've all got their coats. Run along now, you haven't much time, they are moving off at 2.30 p.m.'

I muttered all the way down to the town hall. I thought just how typical of the man that conversation had been. He couldn't come up and tell me straight away that there was a march. Oh no! He's always got to be bloody devious.

I looked at my watch; it was already a few minutes past the half-hour.

I hurried around the last corner and the town hall loomed into sight. I searched intently for 150 protesting teachers. By ten minutes to three, eight of them had turned up. This would give us an escort ratio of one-to-one. The Peckham education offices would think they were receiving a visit from the President of the United States. With escort and marchers now sheltering from the rain, this whole demonstration had the makings of the non-event of the year.

As the rain eased, so the numbers of the demonstrators increased. Finally, at 3.15 p.m., with the ranks of the teachers now swollen to thirty, the organizers decided to move off. Our route would take us past the police station and I had already decided to leave the procession at that point. I contacted Peter Cage on my personal radio, pointing out that the march was ridiculously over-policed and that, together with four other PCs, I intended to leave the procession very soon.

He agreed, although he blamed me for the lack of numbers. He also said: 'If you can come back to the station within the next fifteen minutes, there is a rather charming lady asking to see you, although I can't think why. I have placed her in the waiting-room, so don't be all day.'

I thanked him with mild curiosity and then took up a position at the head of the march.

Now all marches should have a chant. Repetitive and boring they may be, but no march, other than a funeral, should ever be held in silence. The chant leader therefore began to make her first sounds. A high, shrill voice cut through the traffic-laden air.

'WHAT-DO-WE-WANT?' she screeched.

'NO-CUTS!!' roared the twenty-nine in unison.

'WHEN-DO-WE-WANT-THEM?' she persisted.

205

'NOW!!' came back the bewildering response.

I shot a puzzled glance across to my friend and colleague Jim Pierce, who had joined me in leading the procession.

'English teachers,' he explained, confidently. 'If it's a double-negative then they are almost always English teachers.'

Well, Jim was married to a teacher, so I was not prepared to argue with his theory. As the march progressed along the Walworth Road, so the chant leader grew in confidence. Every few yards she would burst into yet another slogan. The voice would become even more shrill as it climbed octave after octave. Her 'WHAT-DO-WE-WANTs?' were cutting into me for the sixth time when I involuntarily winced and looked again at Jim. He in turn gave a few seconds' attention to the lady. After a short study of her, he sidled over to me.

'Have you ever noticed that all screechy-voiced teachers have long tits?'

I had to confess that I had never before noticed that particular phenomenon. However, searching my memory thoroughly for every screechy-voiced teacher that I could remember, I realized that there was a definite abundance of long tits amongst them. I now looked at Jim in a whole new light. I had somehow never before seen him as a thinking man.

Our whole entourage had by this time reached the police station. Jim and I plus two other constables then dropped out of the march and returned to the comparative peace of the station front-office. There Peter Cage allocated each of the group to another task but held me back, saying, 'The bird in the waiting-room looks a real lady; what on earth is she doing with you?'

I pointed out that she was doubtless from the heavy social circle that I move in when I am not compelled to listen to boring old police sergeants, and I entered the waiting-room.

I was immediately delighted to see the smiling face of an old friend. Maude Good was the most aptly named person that I have ever met. She was so serene it was almost sickening. She had the disposition of an angel and the type of lovely rounded face that only plump women seem blessed with. As each year slipped by, so weight would gain a few more pounds. Her jumpers and blouses would bite deeper into her back – and her face would become lovelier. If nature had awarded her the face as a compensation for the rest of her body, then Maude had indeed received a pretty fair bargain. Her main attribute was in fact not her face at all but her real and genuine concern for others. She had been widowed twice and had a handicapped son from her second marriage. Now, as she entered middle-age, the boy had died. This triple tragedy in her life seemed only to equip her better for dealing with other people's problems. These were usually far less harrowing than her own.

We exchanged our usual pleasantries and then she said, 'Could you go and have a word with Mrs Elizabeth Crawley at 96 Lawn Court, Harry? She worries me greatly. She's extremely ill and although she has been in the flat less than a month, she's already having a great problem with the kids.'

'Is she on her own?'

'Yes. I think she's a widow. I'm not too sure how old she is, it is difficult to tell with her being so ill, but I would think she is around seventy-odd.'

I promised Maude that I would do all that I could and as usual her face lit up in gratitude.

That evening, I strolled through Lawn Court in search of number 96. I eventually discovered it to be a ground-floor flat at the end of a terraced row. There was a large raised flowerbed in front of the houses and access could only be gained by walking around this bed and approaching from the side. The door of number 96 was in stark contrast to every other door on the estate. The sparkling varnish stain had been peeled back and the surface of the wood was violated by deep scratches and gouges.

I rapped on the knocker several times but received no reply. I was just about to leave, believing that there was no one at home, when I heard a faint cry.

'Who is it?' said the distant voice.

I bent down and called through the letter-box. 'It's a policeman, Mrs Crawley. It's all right, it's nothing for you to worry about. Can you just open the door for a minute?'

I heard shuffling and panting before the door finally opened. It revealed a very tired, grey-haired and grey-complexioned lady. She was bent forward alarmingly and supported by a gnarled walking-stick. She wore a loose-fitting, badly stained house-coat over a pale blue nightie. A surgical collar was fixed around her neck and just beneath the collar an angry-looking scar disappeared down the top of her nightgown. Her face was puffy and there were grazes across her knuckles. She wore no footwear at all and her semi-toothless mouth gaped open in puzzlement at my call. The evening was chill, yet she sweated profusely, wisps of hair clinging to her forehead.

'I ... can't stand ... here ... talking,' she panted. 'Come ... inside.'

Closing the door, I slowly followed her along a short, linoleumed passage into a surprisingly clean, well-furnished living-room. She practically fell into one armchair and weakly waved me into the other one.

'Yes ... what do you ... want?' she heaved, wincing as if every individual word was a separate fight.

'Well, I understand that you've been having some trouble with kids, luv. I just called around to see if I could help.'

'I'm-I'm ... going ... m-mad here ... They ... torment-torment ... me every ... night ... They carve ... w-w-words ... on ... door ... They ... pour ... paint over ... my-my ... window ... They ... push ... burning ... paper ...

208

through . . . letter . . . box. I . . . am . . . so-so . . . fri-frightened! I . . . keep . . . falling . . . over . . . L-L-Look at . . . my . . . bruises!'

She pulled up the sleeves of her house-coat and displayed great blue areas on her arms. I was appalled. I had experienced many years of dealing with complaints about kids and I thought that I was hardened to it, yet I had never before seen anything as terrifying as this.

'When did this start?' I asked incredulously.

'The first . . . week . . . that . . . I . . . m-m-moved . . . in,' she replied.

'Do you have any relatives nearby?'

'I have . . . a . . . m-m-married . . . son . . . a . . . few . . . miles . . . away. I . . . I . . . also . . . have a . . . d-d-daughter . . . who's . . . a . . . bit mental . . . in . . . a . . . home . . . up . . . n-n-north . . . And I have . . . another . . . daughter . . . in . . . Aus-Australia.'

Eventually, after a long and arduous session, she managed to convey to me the full story of her plight. She was in extremely bad health and had been rehoused from a medium-sized council house in the suburbs at Enfield to this small, one-bedroom flat in Southwark. The house had been suitable for her when her husband was alive and the children were at home but finally it proved much too big. It was also very soon obvious to me that, apart from any aggravation with the local kids, she did not wish to live here anyway.

'But why did the council move you here in the first place? They would not have moved you so far if you weren't agreeable.'

'They . . . told . . . me . . . it . . . would . . . be for . . . the . . . better . . . and . . . I . . . b-b-believed them . . . but . . . I . . . hate . . . it . . . here . . . and . . . I . . . just . . . wish . . . that . . . I . . . had-had . . . never . . . moved . . .' She fell back breathless.

'Why?'

'Cos . . . I . . . don't . . . know-know . . . anyone . . . here . . .'

'Well, you will, you'll just have to give it time.'

'No ... I ... hate ... it! I-I-I ... must ... move ... away ... I-I'm ... terrified ... here. Can't ... you ... help me?'

'I'll make a few phone calls in the morning, luv, and I'll see what I can find out. I'll pop back and see you tomorrow evening, okay?'

'Thank you. I ... m-m-must ... get ... out.'

I saw myself out and took a stroll around the estate before returning to the station to book off-duty. It was very quiet, with hardly a child to be seen. I also decided to stop off and have another look around on my drive home, but that was equally fruitless.

That night I just could not get Mrs Crawley out of my mind. What state had society got itself into when old ladies were in such terror?

I spent much of the next morning on the telephone. Mrs Crawley did have a social worker in Enfield but she had not yet been allocated one since her move to Southwark.

'She will have one in due course and we are most certainly aware of her,' said the voice on the telephone. 'But it takes time and we have been told by Enfield that she has a tendency to exaggerate her circumstances.'

'Exaggerate her circumstances!!' I exploded. 'She's had open-heart surgery and a stroke! She suffers from hardening of the arteries, she can barely walk *and* she wears a surgical collar! How on earth can a seventy-year-old woman exaggerate those circumstances?'

'Did she tell you she was seventy?'

'No. She didn't have to. You can see it.'

'How old do you think she is?'

'I would guess around seventy-three.'

'Well, I wouldn't guess within her hearing, if I was you – she'd probably kill you. She's fifty-two and four months to be precise.'

210

'What!!' I was stunned for a moment. 'Well-well, that just bears out the state of her general health, then, doesn't it?'

'It certainly appears that we should give her some sort of priority. We haven't yet seen her, you understand. All we have to go on at the moment is her file that has been transferred from Enfield.'

'I can take it that you will see her soon, then?'

'Just as soon as we can. We are very busy, you know.'

'Aren't we all, luv.'

My dialogue with the housing department was no more rewarding. Yes, they knew of Mrs Crawley; no, they had no further plans for her. She complained frequently and had been trying to move out almost from the very first day that she had moved in.

That did not tell me anything that I did not know already. Actually, I could not see how the housing office could help much anyway. I fully realized that it was not possible to keep moving people around from house to house. The only way out of this dilemma would be somehow to convince Mrs Crawley that she was quite safe in Lawn Court. But how? Well, there were the kids for a start. I would have to spend a great deal of time in the vicinity in an attempt to resolve that particular problem.

For the next few weeks I practically haunted Lawn Court. It was terribly time-consuming and extremely boring. It would be nice to say it was effective, but it wasn't. The attacks continued. They had no set pattern except that they were between 9 p.m. and 2 a.m. There was more paint, more scratches, more obscenities and more threats through the letter-box. There would be several weeks of total quiet, then the attacks would begin again. The infuriating aspect was that the perpetrators always seemed to be so lucky. I would sit in my car reasonably well concealed for four consecutive evenings and nothing would happen. On the fifth evening, while I had a leave-day, early-turn, or was otherwise employed, the attacks would be renewed, often with such vigour that Mrs Crawley would crash to the floor in sheer terror and remain there all night.

I finally decided that this hit-or-miss approach was useless. A permanent observation would have to be kept each evening until something *did* happen. The maddening thing was that one of Mrs Crawley's neighbours claimed that he had seen the attackers several times. He usually gave a different description of them and claimed that he had actually chased them away one night. I was not impressed with his 'eye-witness' account for several reasons. First, he had difficulty in seeing me when I was standing in front of him. Secondly, the suspect that he chased was allegedly drunk and fell over three times, yet he had still failed to catch him. Thirdly, I felt that he just wanted to be part of the drama. I doubted if he had seen anything at all, although he seemed sincerely to believe he had. In fact, at one stage, I strongly suspected him of the attacks. He always seemed to be around when they were made.

To secure a suitable observation point of the flat was not easy. I had decided not to use my car any more; it was possibly too well known. About fifty yards away from number 96 was a broken-down, derelict van. It had been there for some months and the council had attached a seven-day notice to it. This notice stated that the vehicle would be removed by the council for scrap if it was not removed within that period. The notice was now two months old!

I had asked Dave Dawson, a young PC from the night duty, if he would assist me with the observation. After all, should our attacker leg it, then it would be nice to have someone who could still sprint a little. He agreed and we both made ourselves as comfortable as possible in the two front seats of the old van. In addition to this van, we had another unexpected piece of luck. The street light immediately above us had developed a fault and had failed to illuminate that evening. We were now ideally placed in a nondescript vehicle in a deserted street. We were also partially concealed within the curve of a bend, with a perfect view of Elizabeth Crawley's front door. For the first time for months I was feeling quite optimistic.

The unseasonable early summer temperature began to drop appreciably and we turned up our collars and slumped deeper into our uncomfortable seats. There is nothing like a long observation in a motor vehicle, especially an uncomfortable one, for really exhausting a topic of conversation. Usually the subject is sport. This may marginally edge in front of sex. Little did we realize that tonight we would simply discuss the former, but that we were to take part practically in the latter.

The first couple of hours slipped by very smoothly. Even though our sporting loves were not compatible, mine being football while his was rugby, we found mutual ground with cricket. Even this discussion palled after a while and we slowly slipped into a rarely punctuated silence. Around 11.30 p.m., when the last of the customers from the nearby King's Arms had drifted home, a numbness began to attack my buttocks with the vigour of a dozen dentists.

'I'm gonna have to stretch my legs,' I muttered. 'I'm dead below the hips.'

'Shsssssss,' whispered my young companion. 'There's someone lurking around the side of number 96.'

I stared intently through the filthy windows of the van and I could just discern a movement in the distant shadows.

'I think there are two people,' said Dave, his eyes narrowing in concentration.

I could certainly see two shadows, but the view of Mrs Crawley's front door was partially obstructed by the flowerbed. The figures then moved a couple of yards, then stopped and seemed suddenly to merge into one. Dave reached for the door handle but I restrained him.

'We haven't actually seen anything yet – wait for a minute or so longer.'

He nodded. The two figures then moved closer to us and in fact emerged from the pathway at the side of Lawn Court on to the pavement immediately ahead of us.

'Blast! They've sussed us out!' said the youngster.

'No, they can't have done. These windows are so filthy I doubt if they would be able to see in, even in broad daylight. Just sit still and we will see what develops.'

I again placed a restraining arm upon him and he slowly and reluctantly eased back into his seat. As the shadows neared, so they began to take on definite forms. They were soon apparent to us as a courting couple. A rather ardent and passionate couple at that. The man was totally unknown to me but the woman I recognized instantly as a manageress of a baker's from the nearby Walworth Road.

She was a striking-looking woman who customarily dressed in outfits more suited to her teenage daughter. Tonight was no exception. Her dyed blonde hair contrasted well with her light-blue, short and shiny, PVC raincoat. If she just possibly managed to get away with the coat, then she had gone well over the top with her three-quarter-length, white cowboy boots. They were over-fiddly, with strands of imitation leather hanging untidily down everywhere. There were also other indictments in her appearance. She had doubtless been quite adept with her facial make-up some twenty years earlier. This expertise, now even more proficient, was totally wasted by her insistence on using the same ancient styles. The back-combed hair, the thin, pencil-lined eyebrows, the shiny bacon-lips, then the pan-stick facial paste (with its inevitable tide-mark above the white of the neck), all dated her even more than her thickening

214

waist. None of these faults, however, could be seen in the gloom of that Walworth street. In any case, the two hours spent in the King's Arms would doubtless have convinced her escort that she was Aphrodite.

When the couple were about five yards in front of our vantage point, they stopped for a real rib-crushing embrace. His right hand was placed firmly across her shoulder blades, while his left hand pulled equally firmly on her buttocks. She reacted to this by pushing even harder into him. His left hand then dropped swiftly to the hem of her coat and rose equally fast up underneath it! In response to the hand that was now placed firmly on her bum, she began to eat his face. He obviously loved it.

It was at this interesting stage that they both overbalanced and staggered giggling across the pavement. They quickly leapt back into each other's arms and while he was nuzzling her neck, he appeared to whisper something in her ear. Removing her gaze from his face, she turned her head towards our van. She remained motionless for a few seconds, then, nodding her head in obvious agreement, she kissed him lightly on the lips. They both then turned and walked hand-in-hand towards us!

I guessed instantly what was intended.

'Is your door locked?' I hissed sharply to Dave.

He made no reply but stealthily eased the handle forward. There was a dull clunk. We sank even lower in our seats. The footsteps passed by the front of the vehicle and carried on around to the back. We heard the two back doors opening, and the van tilted as first the man climbed aboard and then the woman. A wooden partition sectioned off the front seats from the rest of the van. There was just a small opening in this partition, presumably for the driver to obtain a rear view. I had a gnawing feeling that a rear view was exactly what we were about to receive.

During the next ten minutes the van rocked and rolled

appreciably. Dave began to giggle but I was quite surprised at my own restraint. Suddenly we heard a crash as if something heavy had fallen. I heard a distinct, masculine oath and I could not resist turning my head to peak through the opening. It was then that I, too, lost control. An oily old spare tyre had been propped against the inside of the vehicle and the vibration had finally toppled it. It had fallen neatly across a puffy, rounded, bare bum. It looked like a winning throw in some Roman orgy hoopla-stall. I suddenly imagined the proprietor's reaction: 'Oh praise the gods, Emperor! You have won a bum! How would you like it? Here, or take away?'

It was the final straw for me. I completely dissolved. The vehicle rocked with even greater intensity as Dave and I infected each other with our laughter. The merriment in the front was equalled only by the panic in the back. There was another crash as the tyre was hurtled across the back of the van.

'I bet it's my old man!' sobbed the manageress.

'What shall we do?' gasped Dave, now with tears in his eyes.

'I don't know,' I responded. 'It's not a situation that happens too often. I think we'll just keep our heads down. I doubt very much if they'll hang about once they get out of the van.'

The banging of the doors and the sounds of running footsteps indicated the accuracy of my observation. Slowly we straightened ourselves up to a more comfortable position. We wiped the inside of the windscreen clear of condensation and resumed our observation.

'Oh no!' exclaimed Dave.

'What is it?' I asked anxiously, all traces of former merriment instantly disappearing.

'Look! Can't you see, man? The door of number 96 – it's on fire!'

We pushed hard on our respective doors, predictably forgetting that we had locked them just a few minutes before. There was a five-fumbling-seconds delay before we both tumbled out into the night air. Dave was away first; my legs were still busily protesting about their long incarceration. On my arrival at the door of number 96, Dave had managed to stamp out the fire. Oil-soaked paper had been piled up around the base of the door and flames had leapt up way past the letter-box. Even in that still air, charred and burnt paper began to swirl rhythmically around.

I pounded repeatedly on the door, afraid that some of the paper had been inserted into the letter-box. The door eventually opened and Elizabeth Crawley practically collapsed into my arms.

'I-I-I heard ... the-them ... It ... was ... awful ... "Let's ... burn ... the ... bitch" they ... said.'

We carried her into the bedroom and returned her to the bed. She appeared to have scars and bruises everywhere. Dave went into the kitchen for a glass of water, while I attempted vainly to console her.

'They ... they'll ... k-k-kill me ... I-I-I ... know ... they ... will ...'

Dave and I spent the next thirty minutes feeling totally inadequate. At one stage, I thought that she had actually stopped breathing. I pressed her chest and although she moaned instantly with pain, her breathing seemed to improve.

'Look, you simply must go to hospital, Mrs Crawley,' I insisted.

'No ... no ... no ... I-I'm all right ... I-I ... tell ... you.'

'Mrs Crawley, you are anything *but* all right! Just let them have a look at you. If they say you are okay, then they'll send you home again. That's sensible, isn't it?'

'N-n-no ... I'm ... due ... at ... hospital ... early ... next ... week. I-I ... won't ... go ... until then ... I-I-I'm

217

... fed ... up ... with ... hospitals ... They ... never ... do ... me ... much ... good anyway.'

We left the flat with the promise that we would let her son know first thing in the morning of her latest troubles.

'I'll sit on that bloody flat every night until I sort this out,' I said determinedly. 'And there is also a strong possibility that I'll set fire to the bastard responsible with his own bloody matches.'

Dave and I again took up residence in the van for the next few nights. We saw neither the lovers nor the fire-raiser. We became progressively more bored. At the back of my mind was the uneasy feeling that we would both fall asleep and wake up to find the whole estate razed to the ground.

I was due for some leave, and eventually I took a few days off. Dave, with the permission of his shift inspector, carried on with the observation in the company of another recruit. This time they managed to secure access to an empty flat which overlooked the whole of Lawn Court. It was a particularly good vantage point. The lads took a flask and a radio and prepared themselves for a long stay.

On my return from leave, I entered the front office and booked myself on duty. Sergeant Cage was station officer that morning.

'Ah ha! The wanderer returns. How come you spend ages round at Lawn Court with sod all to show for it, yet the first day that you are away two young recruits crack it? There's no doubt about it, you're about as sharp as a marble.'

'What! Lawn Court? Did they catch someone? Who was it, how did they catch them?'

'It was an acquaintance of yours, apparently. All your acquaintances are bloody dubious. This one apparently knew you very well. Asked for you by name, in fact. She said she was sure that PC Cole would not try to blame her for it.'

218

'She! D'you mean that *she* was a woman?'

'Well, "shes" usually are.'

'Oh, sod you!'

'Don't be rude to your sergeant, Constable Cole. I'll tell you what. Any time the job becomes a little too much for you again, I'll get a couple of brand-new recruits and they can do it for you. Now off you go, it's time for your lie-down.'

'Aw come on, sarge,' I pleaded. 'Who was it?'

He raised his eyebrows and tilted his chin back. He put on his exceedingly smug look and proceeded to ignore me. I will kill him one day, I really will.

I ran from the office into the canteen. There, surrounded by a mountain of sausage, beans and chips, was Dave Dawson.

'Who was it, Dave?'

He finished his mouthful and put down his fork.

'It was her,' he said softly.

'Not Mrs Crawley, surely?' I said, incredulously.

He nodded. 'She came out of her front door at 2.15 a.m. minus her surgical collar, minus her walking stick *and* minus her limp! She then threw paint all over her kitchen windows and began to gouge chunks out of her door. After a few minutes of that, she placed a pile of old newspapers at the entrance to her flat and set fire to them. She was just about to close the door when we stepped in. She still had the matches in her hand.'

'But why?'

'Well, although I think that she was pretending harassment in an attempt to be rehoused, I also believe she is honestly convinced that she did not do it. She is just two different people. Although I fetched her into the station, at this stage she has yet to be charged. First we could not get anyone out from the council at that time of night to sign the charge sheet and, in any case, that delay was particularly handy. We have bailed her to return here next week. By that time her doctor, the social services, her son and every other bugger who has an interest will have seen her. I think that she may well be unfit to plead. Incidentally, she requested that you go around and see her.'

I shook my head in bewilderment and walked away. An hour or so later, I headed for Lawn Court. Just before midday I arrived outside number 96. The remnants of white paint had now hardened into great broad stripes down the window panes. The scorch marks now ranged practically all over the front door. A large circular oil-stain lay on the ground immediately in front of the flat. The door of the outside cupboard that housed the dustbin had been torn from its hinges. The bin was lying on its side with the contents scattered. The flat that was not yet six months old already had the appearance of a hovel.

I was within five yards of the door when I just knew that I could not bring myself to knock upon it. I turned around and walked sadly back to the police station.

Harry Cole

POLICEMAN'S PROGRESS

Being one of four policemen coping with the drunken, sex-mad, middle-aged, pear-shaped Clara, or sitting out a night with the neighbourhood ghost, or calming wayward Rosie, the local prostitute, who'd had her 'Bristols' bitten, must have been a lot more fun than digging out the late and seventy-year-old Elsie Morton, rotting in bed after not being seen for some weeks, dealing with violence, or bearing the news of fatal accidents to bereaved families.

PC Harry Cole, now nearly thirty years on the Southwark force, has done it all and there's consequently many a tale to tell. He produces his account of life on the beat with a combination of good humour and honesty that makes *Policeman's Progress* a rich mixture of riotous and serious reading. Harry Cole's loyalty to the force, but also his obvious sympathy for all reasonable human eccentricities, make one feel that he would be a good man to have around when there's trouble.

Harry Cole

POLICEMAN'S LOT

It's a policeman's lot to be involved with eccentric human behaviour and bizarre happenings, with personal dramas and social occasions, accidental disasters and deliberate wrong-doings. PC Cole, after nearly thirty years on the beat, has seen it all; and whether he's investigating the case of the exploding sewer cover or refereeing at a drunken Irish party, withstanding the abuse of the Gay Liberation Front or sorting out the imaginary fears of a lonely old man, it's his sense of humour that often seems the saving grace.

Fontana Paperbacks
Non-fiction

Fontana is a leading paperback publisher of non-fiction. Below are some recent titles.

You can buy Fontana paperbacks at your local bookshop or newsagent. Or you can order them from Fontana Paperbacks, Cash Sales Department, Box 29, Douglas, Isle of Man. Please send a cheque, postal or money order (not currency) worth the purchase price plus 22p per book for postage (maximum postage required is £3).

NAME (Block letters) _____

ADDRESS _____

_____

_____